Just Love

Why God must punish sin

Ben Cooper

THE GOOD BOOK COMPANY

Just Love: Why God must punish sin

© Ben Cooper/St Helen's Media 2005

Published by The Good Book Company
Elm House, 37 Elm Road, New Malden, Surrey KT3 3HB
Tel: 020-8942-0880; Fax: 020-8942-0990
E-mail: admin@thegoodbook.co.uk
website: www.thegoodbook.co.uk

ISBN 1-904889-54-9

Cover design Carl Hamblin.
Printed in the UK by Bookmarque

Contents

Before we begin...

IT WAS A GREY, OVERCAST DAY in October 1993. I had met up with my wife Catherine in her lunch-hour, and we were now standing at the door of an ugly modern house rather incongruously set within the grand architecture of central Oxford.

We rang the bell.

It wasn't the first time we'd been there. A few days earlier we'd been standing in exactly the same place. That time, after a long wait, the door had been briskly opened by a large grey-haired man. I think it was Catherine who spoke. I can't remember the exact words she used, but it was something like: 'Hello, we'd like to talk to you about Christianity. We've been thinking about it, and we'd like to find out more'.

He didn't flinch. Sorry, they were in the middle of lunch. Could we come back some other time? We fixed a date, and went away.

So here we were, back again. The same imposing figure opened the door. He looked pleased to see us and bustled us excitedly into the living-room. 'I'm so glad you came back!'

He sat us down, offered us coffee, and handed us a couple of Bibles.

Now I was definitely feeling uncomfortable. I kept thinking, 'What on *earth* am I doing here?' I hadn't even been particularly keen on coming. I was beginning to feel I should have been a little firmer with Catherine—that I should have put a stop to all this nonsense much earlier. It was a feeling like being sucked into some lengthy sales pitch for a dubious time-share deal—a desperate feeling that we should just get out before we were forced into something regrettable.

Neither of us come from Christian families. My parents would probably describe themselves as agnostic, but I grew up in an atmosphere of scepticism about most things, and that certainly covered religion. Both Catherine and I had managed to get through our student years completely oblivious to anything remotely Christian. By my early twenties I would have been happy to call myself an atheist. Catherine might not have put it so strongly, but her views would have been pretty much the same.

We were only here because of Catherine's curiosity about one of her work-colleagues. She was working at the time in a basement laboratory, as a member of a team firing lasers at blobs of atoms. One other member of the team was a Christian. This was novel: neither of us had met a Christian who talked so openly about God and his faith. Over the last two years he had patiently answered our questions and encouraged us to find out more. Even when he moved away to Paris, we continued the discussion by post. We received long letters (the only letters

I've ever received with footnotes!), dealing with my heated objections. Eventually he persuaded us to go and talk to someone else about it, and gave us directions to the house where we were now sitting.

'What do you think happened on the cross?' asked the grey-haired man in the armchair opposite.

We were at a loss to know what to say. What sort of answer was he hunting for? That the man called Jesus was executed? It seemed too obvious. Our mumbled replies made him realise that he needed to start a little further back.

He tried a different tack. 'Do you think it's right,' he asked, 'that people should be punished for the things they do wrong?'

Now that was a question! I can't tell you the complex series of thoughts that went through my head when he asked that. You see, at the time, I was studying economics; indeed, a rather rarefied branch of economics called 'Game Theory', which has plenty to say about why and how people are punished. I was just about to give a classic economist's answer and say, 'Well, it depends...' But I stopped myself and thought for a second. Putting aside all the academic complications, *what did I really think?* Did I *really* think that it's right for people to be punished for the things they do wrong? Well, maybe—certainly sometimes. Hesitantly, I said so.

He nodded, and then got us to open the Bibles he had given us. And he explained what had happened on the cross.

God must punish wrong-doing. God must punish sin, he explained. Many people have a view that God is 'just love' in a way that means he will not punish sin, he said. But to truly understand the love of God, we need to understand that God is also *just*. I didn't really get it then—not in any depth. It felt at the time that I could so easily have argued against it. Indeed,

I could have argued in a rather sophisticated way against it. I could have argued in such a way as to have left this man, with his slightly manic look and his Bible in his hands, high and dry, baffled by the technicalities of modern approaches to the theory of punishment.

But (thank God) I didn't. I understood enough to know that, whatever the textbooks and theorists say, I, Ben Cooper, desperately needed God's forgiveness. I understood enough to see that God could not just forget about the wrong stuff in my life—that he had to deal with it. So, for the first time in my life, and against every instinct, I prayed. On that day in October 1993, I prayed that God would forgive me. And Catherine followed a few minutes after. We had been married for three years. Nothing now would ever quite be the same again.

★ ★ ★

Why I wrote this book...

Many years on from that day, I now realise that the struggles I had to understand this basic fact about God are not mine alone. Many people wrestle with the question of justice in this world and the next. How is it that a God who is revealed to us as the source and essence of love can *also* be a judge who punishes wrongdoers? The question and its answer in the Bible is not, at one level, hard to understand, but the implications for us are enormous. This book was born out of my own struggles with this issue, and my growing awareness that it is an area of what God says about himself in the Bible that many people have similar difficulties with.

I am specifically writing for three kinds of people.

If you are **unconvinced** by the claim that God must punish sin, then you *could* read on to confirm your scepticism. You might write me off as someone trying to defend a rather crazy decision he made some time ago—to save face. I hope you don't. Because if your scepticism is that strong, then I wonder if there is *anything* I could say to change your mind. As a sceptic, you'll always be able to come up with some psychologically plausible story to explain my strange set of beliefs.

Although, if your scepticism is *that* strong, I might also wonder how you manage to function in life at all. When you wake up, your eyes are trying to persuade you that you're lying in your bedroom. But you doubt it. It's probably an illusion generated by some mad scientist who has your brain bottled in his Transylvanian laboratory. Scepticism at this level can really mess your life up.

If you are approaching this book as a sceptic, then let me encourage you to read on *doubting your doubts*. Why not take this opportunity to re-examine the way you look at the world? Why not allow yourself to be challenged and provoked? If your current way of looking at things is well-founded, then reading with an open mind should hold no fears for you. But let me also be honest with you about my intentions: my hope is that you will come to believe, as I did, that you need forgiveness from God. And my prayer is that you find it.

On the other hand, you might be someone **genuinely curious** about the Christian faith. Perhaps you've already started investigating. And there's much you've seen and heard that you've found very attractive, except... Well, except this whole subject. You're surprised by how often when you dip into the Bible you're confronted by an angry God, a God acting in judgment and punishment. And you're troubled by the fact that Jesus, whom in many ways you find compelling, seems to buy into this big theme of judgment. What's more, many committed Christians tell you that this aspect of the faith, far from being a optional extra, is right at the heart of things.

If that's you, then I hope this book will be an opportunity for you to think through the whole issue. How does the God who acts in punishment fit with the God who is love? If the fact that God is love means that he is 'just love', how can he ever punish anyone? What does it mean to say that someone deserves punishment? For what purpose does God act in punishment? What does it achieve? Those are some of the issues we shall be tackling in the course of this book. And we shall be taking a close look at some carefully reasoned explanations of why God must punish sin.

You may, alternatively, read this book a third way. You may read it as someone who would already describe yourself as a **Christian** but who yet remains deeply uncomfortable about the Bible's picture of a God who punishes sin. You're well aware that many people describing themselves as Christian flatly deny it and might even say it was anti-Christian. And if there's one aspect of the Christian message that you're tempted to feel ashamed of it's this. You're happy to talk to your friends about a relationship with Jesus, about the way of love and self-sacrifice—but *this...*

For you, my hope and prayer is that reading this book will restore your confidence that this idea is the truth. And that, being persuaded that our loving Father in heaven is also the judge who will punish sin, you will find a boldness to defend it. And, God-willing, you should be able to say why.

'Must'?

I ought to get straight exactly what it is I'm hoping to show you from what God says about himself in the Bible. It's this: God is not 'just love' in a way that smothers his determination to punish sin. Rather, God's love is a just love. God *must* punish sin. My claim is that this is what God says and argues himself. It is, largely speaking, a fairly straightforward claim. 'Sin', for the moment, we can take to be a way of talking about wrong-doing. Punishing wrongdoing is hardly an unfamiliar idea. And it doesn't take much reading in the Bible to find God frequently punishing wrong-doing, or warning that he will punish it. That God does punish wrong-doing is fairly plain.

But to claim that God *must* punish sin is profoundly different. And we need to be clear what we *don't* mean by that, as well as what we do.

What I certainly don't mean in saying that God must punish sin is this: I don't mean that there is something external to God which *makes* him punish sin—to suggest that God is *under* some 'force', 'law' or 'rule' that is in some way greater than him. As I will emphasise repeatedly, God is dependent on nothing and no-one.

What I do mean when I say 'God must punish sin' is this. **Given what it is possible to know about God, we cannot rightly conceive of him doing anything else. Anything other than *always* punishing *every* act of sin.** I mean that it would be out of character, inconsistent, even weird, for him not to punish sin. God never acts out of character, and it's in that sense that he 'must' do things consistent with his character. That's what I mean by 'God *must* punish sin'.

We all see something like this in everyday life. For people I know very well, I can say with some certainty things they will always do or will never do. I can think of someone whose arachnophobia means I can safely assert that she will never keep a tarantula as a pet. People we know are never entirely consistent, of course, and I guess that one day she could surprise me. Not so with God. He makes statements about himself that carry a great degree of certainty; which means that, in principle at least, we can make statements about him that also suggest a high degree of certainty.

This is one of the reasons why the Bible will play a central role in the arguments of this book. How can we get to know God well enough to make such assertions about him? To know him well enough to make a claim as strong as 'he *must* punish sin'? Well, it is God's own claim in the Bible that it is through the Scriptures that he engages with people and speaks to them. I simply don't have the space to defend that fully here, except to say that we quickly run into problems finding any *other* way of coming to know God.* If we rely on anything less or anything more than the whole Bible then we run into huge problems trying to identify what is and what isn't the authentic voice of God. You may well find the references to biblical books in what follows occasionally hard going if you're not used to doing that. But be assured that they are not there out of some sort of 'knee-jerk' fundamentalism. There are very good reasons for taking the Bible as the trustworthy speech of God. As words through which we can get to know him—truly, if not exhaustively.

Why it matters so much

Another thing we ought to get straight before we begin is just how much is at stake here.

---

*For an thoughtful investigation of this issue, you could try *Why believe the Bible?* by John Blanchard.

Let me present you with a betting proposition. It comes from Blaise Pascal, a terribly clever French thinker, and it is sometimes known as 'Pascal's wager'. Pascal was one of those rather annoying people who are stunningly good at everything they turn to. In the seventeenth century he made ground-breaking contributions to analytical geometry, physics and the theory of probability; he even made one of the first mechanical calculating machines. While meditating on philosophy and religion, Pascal proposed a bet that went something like this: Suppose God exists. If you bet for God and believe in him, then you'll receive an unimaginably huge reward in heaven. Unless you think it utterly impossible that God exists, he argued, it then makes sense to bet for him.

Similarly, if you *do not* bet for God and ignore him, then you will receive an unimaginable punishment in hell. Again, unless you think it utterly impossible that God exists, it makes sense to wager for him.

In other words, you would be mad not to 'bet' on God by believing in him, given the upside of belief and the downside of unbelief. As they say in the States it's a no-brainer.

Some people think *Pascal's wager* is frightfully clever. However, if you wouldn't describe yourself as a Christian, I don't suppose you're now thinking, 'Wow, I never thought of it like that before! I think I *will* believe in God!' Clever as it is, I don't suppose you're persuaded.

But why not? I suppose the answer is that we tend to treat the idea of huge rewards in heaven or a terrible punishment in hell as *effectively* impossible—as too unlikely to matter. We put them in the same category as suddenly discovering that you are next in line for the throne, or being hit by an asteroid on the way to the shops, or being swallowed by the office photocopier at work. (Although my own experience with photocopiers suggests that we may be wise to be more cautious here!) With the rewards and punishments too unlikely to matter, we can treat Pascal's wager as merely an interesting philosophical discussion—and that, indeed, is the way people have treated it ever since he raised it.

Imagine a wonderfully civilised scene: a group of friends are enjoying an animated conversation around some fine food and wine. Someone innocently mentions the recent increases in armed crime that headed the news that day. The discussion occupies the next ten minutes: some people being deliberately controversial; some occasionally chipping in with a witty remark; others just keeping quiet and enjoying the banter. But the occasion would have a very different feel, I would guess, if the original questioner drew out a hand-gun and threatened to shoot the entire company.

That's the sort of danger I want to warn you about as we begin this book. We're going to argue about whether God must punish sin. We could proceed as if this were merely some abstract discussion about the character of God. But that would be deceptive. If you are actually persuaded by the arguments in this book, then be warned that things will suddenly get very personal. Like the moment when someone unexpectedly pulls a gun on you, you'll be staring a life and death situation in the face.

If you're persuaded by the arguments in this book, then a whole host of things may change. What you think about yourself may change. What you think about what happened on the cross may change. You may change what you think about what it means to be 'saved' by God. Most of all, perhaps, what you think about that decision whether to 'bet' for God may change. When you read about 'Pascal's wager' you may have thought I was being flippant—treating God and belief on the same level as buying a scratchcard. But suppose you were persuaded that God will act in punishment against each and every act of sin. Persuaded that, far from being 'too unlikely to matter', it is *an absolute certainty that it will happen.*

If you were persuaded of that, then suddenly it becomes a very serious decision indeed.

1. Into the Fray

IN SHAKESPEARE'S *Henry V*, on the night before the battle of Agincourt, the King disguises himself as an ordinary officer. He wants to know the state of his troops. He wants to know their morale the night before a battle in which they will face an army far better equipped and far greater in number. As he wanders in the chill of the night, talking to people from every class and station, the sense of foreboding and fear is heavy in the night air. The scene ends with him praying against the terror that threatens to paralyse his troops, knowing full well that when they see the size of the opposition, the sight is likely 'to pluck their hearts from them'.

Well, like brave King Harry, it's time to face up to the strength of the opposition.

The aim of this short chapter is to be honest about the many strong objections that have been made to the claim that God's love is a *just* love—that he must punish sin. I want to state them as clearly and fairly as possible, and then to suggest how the rest of the book will address these objections.

The main objections are these: First, God is love. Second, he can simply write-off sin like a debt. Third, for him to punish just because someone 'deserves it' seems pointless.

God is love

'God *must* punish sin.' How could anyone say such a thing? God is love. Is a loving God going to subject people he created to pain and suffering? Can we imagine a God who is love being determined to exercise *vengeance or retribution?*

This is probably the most emotive objection. The author of a recent book argues that the rhetoric of judgement and punishment in Christian teaching has masked the fact that God *defines* himself as love. It is indeed true that John categorically states 'God is love' in the first of his letters in the New Testament. We're going to think about that at greater length in the next chapter, but if 'God is love' means that God is 'love only', then we have the ultimate rebuttal to the claim that God must punish sin. Surely, if God *defines* himself as love—not anger, power or judgment, but *love*—then that *must* over-ride everything else? Everything in the Bible must be read, tempered, understood and interpreted through the 'lens' that God is love. Anything that might suggest his determination to punish sin has to be seen against his *greater* determination to act in love.

Sin can be written-off like a debt

The second objection is more subtle: We claim that God must punish sin. But surely, many people will say, it is God's right *not* to punish sin. Why can he not just let people off? To say that God *must* punish sin sounds very much like God is obliged by something or someone else to punish sin. If so, what is it? Why does it have the authority to compel God to act a certain way?

Or the objection can be put more positively: Rather than thinking of God as being at the mercy of some mechanical, impersonal relationship between sin and punishment, isn't it better to think about sin in a more relational way? A recent official document from one the major denominations put it like this: The authors say that our best instincts should lead us to 'personal analogies' to make best sense of the how God deals with sin. Analogies such as, 'Loving parents will often waive a debt owed to them by a child'.*

So, the objection goes, isn't it better to think of God as a creditor with the absolute right to cancel the debt of our sin? Surely, when God 'forgives' us, two things are going on. On the one hand, we the debtors are freed from obligation. On the other, God the creditor does not want to receive what we owe. Now God does forgive, we know that for sure. But since, as he forgives us, he doesn't want to receive what we owe, since he has chosen not to, where's the sense in the notion that he must punish us?

What's the point of punishment?

The final major objection to the claim that God must punish sin asks us to think about the *purpose* of punishment. While the feeling that someone simply 'deserves' to be punished is obviously a common one, what does that actually mean? It might make us feel better to act in vengeance or retribution when it seems someone 'deserves' to be punished, but what does that actually achieve? And how can it be said to achieve justice?

---

* *The Mystery of Salvation: The Story of God's Gift,* a Report by the Doctrine Commission of the General Synod of the Church of England (London, Church House Publishing, 1995), page 212.

Like the others, this is a deeply held objection for some people. Indeed, it is so deeply held in academic circles that very little credence is given any more to the idea of punishment as retribution. If punishment has any purpose, so it is said, it is to deter other potential offenders. Or it is to rehabilitate the offender.

So, to put the objection another way, to say that 'God must punish sin' implies that he punishes merely because they 'deserve it'. But not only does this seem cold and mechanical, it is also purposeless and at odds with any well-respected understanding of punishment today. And punishment seems especially purposeless when we talk about punishing people whom most of us would regard as essentially 'good' people. What's the point of that?

Marshalling a response

If you strongly object to the claim that God's love is a *just* love, that he *must* punish sin, then I may not have yet quite managed to articulate your particular objection. But I think you'll agree that I have raised a formidable number to deal with.

I am going to deal with these objections by pursuing a series of related *arguments*. These are not arguments plucked from thin air. They come from what God says in the Bible about himself and the world we live in.

Arguments can sometimes seem cold and hard, like the logic of *Star Trek's* Dr Spock, but there's no reason why argument should have to displace passion, feeling and emotion. I am aiming to *persuade* you about something. And not just persuade your mind, but also your heart and emotions (if such things are separable, which I'm not sure they are).

Most of the arguments which follow are aimed at dealing with the last of the objections we've just looked at. They are intended to persuade you that there is a real point to God acting in punishment. They are intended to show you *why* God must punish sin. We'll do this in separate chapters looking at our own outrage at wrong-doing; at the fact that God is Creator, that he is LORD and that he is perfectly good.

But we'll begin by dealing with the first two objections. We'll begin with an argument which shows that God's determination to punish sin is fully compatible with his love. It's an argument which also shows that God can't simply 'write off' sin like a debt. And it starts from the same point as the first objection: with the fact that *God is love...*

2. God is Love

IT'S SOMETIMES SAID THAT people don't like abstract ideas. They like things concrete and practical. But that's certainly not true when it comes to love. People love the idea of love.

The index of my *Dictionary of Quotations* has several pages devoted to 'love'. 'How many ways can we express our love of love?' 'Brief is life but love is long.' 'Love is heaven and heaven is love. Virgil said: 'Love carries all before him: we too must yield to love'. (That's Virgil the Roman poet, not the pilot of *Thunderbird 2!*)

And 'Love carries all before him' in many discussions about the character of God. This is what one writer has recently said about God's love:

> The Bible never defines God as anger, power or judgment—in fact it never defines him as anything other than love... The fact is, however else God may have revealed himself, and in whatever way he interacts with the world he has created, everything is to be tempered, interpreted, understood and seen through the

one primary lens of God's love. We should never speak of any
other attribute of God outside the context of his love.*

To say that this is a popular view about God would be an
understatement. God is love. That, surely, is the climax of all
that is revealed about him in the Bible? That, surely, is the
'lens' through which we should interpret everything that's said
about him?

Indeed, if it were up to us to choose the sort of God we would
like, that's the sort of God we might choose. Essentially, 'just
love', nothing but love—everything else one might say about
him swamped by his love. That would be very simple. That
would be very convenient.

And, indeed, we do find God 'defined' by love, in the sense
that in 1 John chapter 4, John tells us that 'God is love.'
Although it might be better, as we shall see, to say that John
means love is defined by God, rather than the other way round.

But it is certainly *not true* to say that this is the only 'God is
...' statement in the Bible. Even earlier in the same letter, we
find John saying 'God is light', referring to his holiness and
moral purity. Elsewhere in the Bible God is the LORD, a merciful God, gracious and merciful, our salvation, our refuge, faithful, a 'sun and a shield'. He is great, greater than all gods,
greater than man, mighty, exalted in power, clothed with terrible majesty, the king of all the earth. He is spirit. He is one. He
is holy, a righteous judge, a consuming fire.

---

* Steve Chalke and Alan Mann, *The Lost Message of Jesus* (Grand Rapids,
Zondervan, 2004), page 63.

Indeed, the descriptions of God as a 'consuming fire', referring to his terrible and inescapable punishment against wickedness, outnumber the phrase 'God is love' *by nine to two*.

That does leave us with some sorting out to do of course. How can we say simultaneously 'God is love' and 'God is a consuming fire'? Are those not mutually exclusive ideas? Well, not necessarily. They might be two perspectives on the same reality.

I don't know much about sculpture. But I do know that when you go to a sculpture gallery, you're supposed to walk around a sculpture and see it from many different points of view. That is, in the few minutes before I get bored and head off for the café.

And many different perspectives is what the Bible gives us on the character of God. But it's not as if we can pick and choose between them. We can't say, 'Oh, I think I'll have the love aspect, thank you—that will do nicely'. People do try to do that, of course. But it can't be right. Just as a sculpture has an underlying unity even though you can look at it from various different angles, so God has an underlying unity. God is one. From one perspective we're told he is a consuming fire; from another, he is love.

The question is: how can anger and love go together? Perhaps we need to look a bit more closely at what love really is...

There's a huge amount in the Bible about God's love. But the phrase 'God is love' only appears in one passage of 1 John; in chapter 4, verses 8 and 16. And when we look at that passage closely, we'll see that a proper understanding of love depends on understanding God's determined opposition to our sins. God's opposition to our sins is so strong that he even sent his only Son to deal with the problem. And as we reflect on the sheer depth of God's love that implies, we shall see our first and most conclusive argument that God must punish sin.

What John says about God's love

Let's look at those two places where the expression 'God is love' appear in the Bible. The first is this:

> Beloved, let us love one another, for love is from God, and whoever loves is from God, and whoever loves has been born of God and knows God. Anyone who does not love does not know God, because God is love. In this the love of God was made manifest among us, that God sent his only Son into the world, so that we might live through him. In this is love, not that we loved God but that he loved us and sent his Son to be the propitiation for our sins. Beloved, if God so loved us, we also ought to love one another. **1 John 4 v 7-11**

And the second comes just a few verses later...

> ...So we have come to know and to believe the love that God has for us. God is love, and whoever abides in love abides in God, and God abides in him. By this is love perfected in us, so that we may have confidence on the Day of Judgment, because as he is so also are we in this world. There is no fear in love, but perfect love casts out fear. For fear has to do with punishment, and whoever fears has not been perfected in love. We love because he first loved us. **1 John 4:16-19**

The context here, as you can see from the first quotation, is that John wants his readers to love each other. And, as people who love one another, and people who have been loved by God, he wants them to have the assurance that they do indeed 'abide in God' and have eternal life. You can see that in the second quotation. It's worth remembering that context. We'll come back to it towards the end of the book.

But to encourage them in all that, John wants them to understand how God first loved them. That is, John's purpose in this letter depends upon his readers understanding how God's love is most powerfully expressed. And we find John's main account of that in verses 9 and 10. Here they are again:

> In this the love of God was made manifest among us, that God sent his only Son into the world, so that we might live through him. In this is love, not that we loved God but that he loved us and sent his Son to be the propitiation for our sins. **1 John 4:9-10**

So in both sentences, God shows his love by sending his Son. But to do what? Well, we can pick out two things from what John says:

- He sent his only Son so that we might live.
- He sent his only Son to be the 'propitiation' for our sins.

These are the things that demonstrate God's love.

God sent his only Son 'to die for us'

For the moment, I want to concentrate on the second of those two points. God sent his Son to be what John calls 'the propitiation for our sins'. 'Propitiation' is some sort of sacrifice that involves death. That is, when John says God sent his Son to be a 'propitiation', it means that he sent Jesus to die.

We can put it in a picture like this:

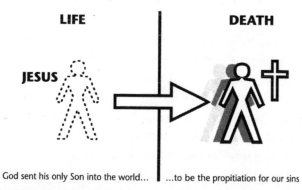

God sent his only Son into the world... ...to be the propitiation for our sins

He sent his only Son

So John says that 'God is love' *because he even went so far as to send his Son to die*. That was an act of such love that it defines what love is.

Over the years Christian preachers have come up with many ways of illustrating what John says about the extent of God's love—given that he sent his Son to die. One of the most powerful is a story about a man and his son in the American South. It's about a bridge-keeper on the Mississippi, whose job it is to operate a lifting bridge for the passing river traffic. One day a riverboat, travelling very fast towards the bridge, signals for it to be lifted. The man is just about to do that when his son calls out, asking if he can help. The man waits, and his son runs towards the bridge. But as he gets close, his son trips and falls down into the bridge lifting mechanism. And he's stuck there.

The riverboat is getting closer and closer, and the bridge-keeper has to make a horrifying decision. Either he goes to rescue his son, and the riverboat crashes into the bridge, possibly killing hundreds of people. Or he lifts the bridge to save them, and crushes his own son to death.

He grits his teeth and lifts the bridge...

It's a very emotive illustration. But it's an appropriate illustration, I believe, because the pattern is exactly the same as we find in John's letter. The bridge-keeper gives up his son for the sake of others. That is his expression of love for the people on that boat. No illustration is perfect, but this one does drive home something of the sheer cost to God in sending his Son to die, and how much he must therefore love the people Jesus dies for.

But the point I want to make from the story of the bridge-keeper is very simple: unless it were absolutely necessary, *he would not have crushed his son to death*. If the bridge-keeper loves his son, then there's no way he's going to casually throw his son's life away for no good reason.

And as John tells us: God sent his Son into the world to die. Indeed, his only Son. The point is the same: *Unless it were absolutely necessary, God would not have sent his only Son to die.*

There *must* have been some very good reason for God to send his Son to die.

Taking the punishment for sin

There must have been a very good reason for God to send his Son to die. But what was it? Many of the reasons people sometimes suggest seem woefully inadequate. Would God have sent his Son to die just to set us an example of obedience, for example? Or just to show that he wants to identify with peoples' suffering? Undoubtedly, Jesus' death on the cross does set us an example of obedience, and it does show God identifying with peoples' suffering. Surely, though, if God sent his *only Son,* there must be more to it than that?

Let's go back to John's statement that God sent his only Son as the 'propitiation' for people's sins. We've said that a 'propitiation' is some sort of sacrifice that involves death. But I'd like to suggest that when John says God sent his Son to die for people's sins it means Jesus was taking *the punishment for their sins.* And there are a number of reasons for that...

1. Death is a punishment

Even the simple fact that Jesus died tells us a great deal about what was happening to him. As we shall see in the chapter *God is Creator*, death only exists in the world because it is the ultimate punishment for sin. So when Jesus died, we know he was *taking the punishment* for sin.

In 2004 Mel Gibson caused a stir with his film *The Passion of the Christ.* What made this extended visual account of Jesus' death so notorious was its emphasis on the gory details of Jesus' physical suffering before his death. But this emphasis is in stark contrast with the accounts of Jesus' death in the New Testament, where there are virtually no gory details at all. These kind of details are not needed. The mere fact that Jesus died shows that he was taking full brunt of the punishment for sin.

2. More about the word 'propitiation'

Propitiation—it's not the sort of word you casually drop into everyday conversation. But it would have made instant sense to the people John was writing to, who would have known their Bibles rather better than we do. It means a sacrifice, a death, that satisfies God's justice.

One of the central problems in the Old Testament is the question of how it was that a holy and perfect God could, to some limited extent, live in the midst of a very imperfect people. God's answer to this question was the sacrificial system that lay at the heart of Israel's worship. An animal had to die to make 'propitiation' for the lives of the people who identified with it. In effect, it bore the punishment for sin on their behalf. (If you're interested, one example you could look up is in Leviticus chapter 5, verses 17 to 19.)

In God's plan, these sacrifices could not actually take away sin. After all, how can an *animal* stand in the place of a *human*? The New Testament reveals that they were but a *picture* of the *real* propitiating sacrifice that deals with the problem of sin, which is what John is telling us about in his letter. He tells us that God sent his Son into the world as the propitiation for our sins. So it's reasonable to conclude therefore that Jesus was sent to take the ultimate punishment for sin.

3. More about the removal of punishment

We get further confirmation about the relation between the death of Jesus and the punishment of sin when we read on in John's letter to his second statement that 'God is love'. 'God is love,' says John, 'and whoever abides in love abides in God, and God abides in him.' But, again, John is keen to remind his readers *what it actually means* for God's love to be expressed in them:

> By this is love perfected in us, so that we may have confidence on the Day of Judgment, because as he is so also are we in the world. There is no fear in love, but perfect love casts out fear. For fear has to do with punishment, and whoever fears has not been perfected in love. 1 John 4:17-18

John has already told his readers that God's love is expressed as he sends his Son to die for their sins. Now he explains further. That death will give him and them confidence on 'the Day of Judgment'. We shall talk about the Day of Judgment at greater length in the chapter God is Good. But even here we can see something of what's involved. Confidence on the Day of Judgment means having no fear of being punished for our sins, because that punishment has already been taken.

Preparations for a big occasion are often a cause of great anxiety. I know, for example, that although it will be very exciting if one of my daughters ever get married, there will also be plenty of things to go wrong. The truth is, I know I'm pretty hopeless at preparing for such occasions. No doubt I'll be asked to do something, and there's a frighteningly high probability that I'll make a mess of it. The day will be approaching, and suddenly my heart will sink as I remember I've forgotten to book the caterers. And I'll crawl heavy-hearted to my wife to confess it. But, knowing her, there's also a very good chance that she, in her long-suffering way, will just say, 'Don't worry—I've done it'. And my fear about everything going wrong on the day will be gone... At least, that's what I'm hoping.

And John is saying that fear has been 'cast out' by love. Our fear of being punished on the Day of Judgment has been cast out by the love of God. The love of God that sent his Son to die has cast it out. 'Don't worry,' says God through John, 'I've done it'. The punishment has been taken.

Gethsemane

We've said that if God sent his only Son to die, it must have been *absolutely necessary* for him to do that. And when we look more closely at the reason John gives the people he's writing to, it seems that God sent his Son to take the punishment for their sins. But are we relying too much here on a trick of logic? A fancy argument? Let's look at one more incident to seal the case.

In the hours running up to the death of Jesus, all of the Gospel accounts describe Jesus going with his disciples to a place called Gethsemane. Asking his closest disciples to watch and pray, he goes to pray himself. Matthew's account has him using these words: 'My Father, if it be possible, let this cup pass from me; nevertheless, not as I will, but as you will'. He prays the same thing three times, clearly aware of what he's just about to face. And then he goes to his death.

By using the word 'cup', Jesus is alluding to a whole stream of Old Testament images. The 'cup' he talks about signifies the 'cup' given by God to people he punishes. It's something that expresses his deep opposition and anger at their sin.

But here, is it possible for the punishment to be taken away? Jesus is praying to his Father, knowing that his Father loves him with a perfect love. Is it absolutely necessary for him to drink the cup, to face the punishment of death? Jesus prays three times, asking for it to be taken away if at all possible. Then he goes willingly to his death. Clearly it is absolutely necessary for him to take the punishment.

Love or child abuse?

What we've seen so far is this: John has told the people he's writing to that God sent his only Son 'as the propitiation for our sins'. God wouldn't have done that unless it were absolutely necessary. There must have been a good reason. And the reason John gives is this: As Jesus died, God was punishing sin in him—not his own sin. We haven't said anything yet about what we can deduce from that. We haven't yet demonstrated that therefore God must punish sin. But we're not far off.

To show you how we're going to complete this argument, I want to return to the story about the bridge-keeper and his son. In the story, a riverboat is steaming full speed towards a closed bridge. The bridge-keeper's son is trapped in the lifting mechanism for the bridge. The only way the bridge-keeper can save the people on the boat from death is by crushing his son.

But what if the story went like this: suppose the bridge is already half-open, and that the riverboat isn't actually in any danger... But that the bridge-keeper pulls the lever and crushes his son anyway.

Or here's a second alternative: suppose the bridge is down but the bridge-keeper's son doesn't trip and fall, but his father suddenly and completely randomly pushes him into the lifting mechanism, forcing himself to make that horrifying decision. And he lifts the bridge to save the people on the riverboat, and crushes his son.

Under either variation, we no longer have a story of heroic, sacrificial love. In either case, we have what amounts to a story that is horrifying for a different reason—it becomes a repulsive and absurd story. It's impossible, surely, to think of a loving father acting like that towards his son? That, surely, would be the very worst sort of child abuse—crushing your son to death when it wasn't necessary?

My argument, then, is this: If the riverboat were in no danger, *then the bridge-keeper would never have let his son die.* He certainly wouldn't have *arranged* for his son to die. He wouldn't have let his son die unless it were *absolutely necessary.* If you have children, think about it. It's hard to think of any circumstances in which you would allow a child of yours to die. There would certainly have to be very, very good reasons. In our story, unless the bridge-keeper were some sort of monster, we can at least say that the riverboat must have been in very serious danger for him to have done what he did.

And it is just the same with the death of God's only Son. If people weren't in danger from their sins, then God wouldn't have sent his Son to die. He wouldn't have let his Son die unless it were absolutely necessary. So people must be in danger from their sins.

And since Jesus was taking their punishment as he died, we can see that they must be in danger of punishment for their sins.

But must he punish everyone?

It should be clear: would God have sent his Son to face a punishment-taking death if there were no need for the punishment to be taken? But let me clear up one last objection you might have: have we shown that God must punish *every* person's sins? In the riverboat example, the bridge-keeper might have let his son die even if, say, only half the people were in danger from the boat hitting the bridge. Similarly, the fact that Jesus died might only show that *some* people are in danger from their sins.

Earlier in his letter John has said that: 'If we say we have not sinned, we make him a liar, and his word is not in us.' So when he now says that God's Son has died for 'our sins', he *must mean* 'the sins of each and every one of us'. For all the people John is writing to, then, we can say this for certain: *God must punish their sins*. But rather than punish them, he punished their sins in his Son.

But there's nothing particularly special about the people John's writing to. Nothing to suggest that these people needed to be punished for their sins in a way that others need not. Indeed, what we read elsewhere in the Bible confirms that the problem facing these people is the problem that faces us all. If it's true for these people that God must punish their sins, then it's true for everyone. We can say more generally: God must punish sin.

Or, if you're still not convinced, let's approach it a different way: in the chapter on *God is Creator*, we're going to look at the solemn promise God made to punish sin with death, a promise made when he established the world in which we live. Think about what God knew when he made that promise. He knew that if he made that promise, the only way he could save anyone from death would be to send his only Son to die on their behalf. But binding himself with a promise when it wasn't necessarily would make him like the bridge-keeper cruelly and unnecessarily pushing his Son into the lifting mechanism of the bridge. So we can say this: *Unless it were absolutely necessary*, God would not have made that promise. For some reason, it was absolutely necessary to promise to punish sin. God must punish sin.

Putting all the pieces together

And at the beginning of the chapter we picked out two aspects of what John says to the people he's writing to:

• He sent his only Son so that we might live.
• He sent his only Son to be the 'propitiation' for our sins.

We've spent some effort looking at the second of those ideas, which can be represented in the diagram below:

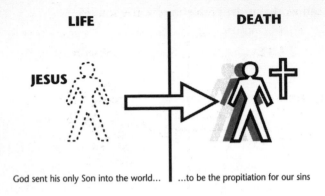

God sent his only Son into the world... | ...to be the propitiation for our sins

But let's add to that the first statement, that God sent his Son 'so that we might live', to get a complete picture of the solution:

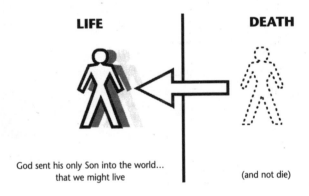

God sent his only Son into the world... that we might live | (and not die)

I suggested earlier that if God sent his only Son into the world to die there must have been a very good reason for it. Now, with the complete picture before us, we can see the extent of what that death achieved. Not only did God send his Son to take the punishment on behalf of sinful humans, he did it *to give them life*. In our story about the bridge-keeper and his son, the bridge-keeper wants the people on the riverboat to live. In the same way, we read in the Bible that God wants to save people *to live—* to live with him forever.

We can work out the problem from the solution:

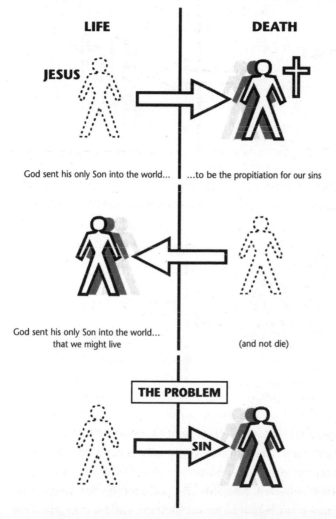

John has told us the solution to our problem: 'God sent his Son into the world to die for our sins so that we might live and not die'. So what's the problem? The problem is that sin is punished with death.

When God gives life, is he cancelling a debt?

According to some people, the statement 'God is love' means that God won't punish. But we've seen that you can only say that if you rip 'God is love' out of its context in the New Testament. To understand the nature and character of God's love depends upon acknowledging that *God must punish sin*. God is not 'just love' in a way that does away with the need to punish of sin. His love is a just love—which remains determined to punish sin.

John's insight also refutes the idea that if we think of sin as a debt to God, then he has the right simply to cancel it. Full stop. So that there's no 'must' about punishing debtors at all.

Now it's quite true that the New Testament authors do talk about sin as a debt and do compare forgiving sin to cancelling a debt. But it's relatively rare, and certainly not the only way they talk about sin and forgiveness. The place where the debt picture is most strongly stressed is probably the parable of the unforgiving servant in Matthew's gospel, which is discussed in a short appendix at the end of this book. All things considered, it's difficult to argue that the New Testament writers are saying that forgiving sin actually is the canceling of a debt contract. The focus in these debt metaphors seems to be on the divine cost in providing forgiveness, and on the liberating effects of forgiving sin—comparable to a release from slavery or debt. When in later chapters we consider the more literal biblical descriptions of sin as rebellion, unbelief and disobedience, it will no longer be at all obvious that God can simply ignore it.

Given what we've seen in this chapter, there must be more to forgiving sin than simply canceling a debt. God sent his only Son to die. There *must* be more to giving people life where otherwise there would be death than something like the casual stroke of an accountant's pen.

The clinching argument

This is only the third of eight chapters, but already we have probably seen the clinching argument that God must punish sin. If you already describe yourself as a Christian, and can see the central importance of Jesus' death on the cross, then this may be the argument you find most persuasive. As we look at Jesus' death, we can know with absolute certainty that God must punish our sin with death. If God could have given us life without sending his Son to die on our behalf, then would he not have done so? So it was absolutely necessary for God to send his Son to die on our behalf. But that only makes sense if it is also absolutely necessary for God to punish our sin with death.

One last diagram to show where we've got to (and we'll keep coming back to this picture throughout the book):

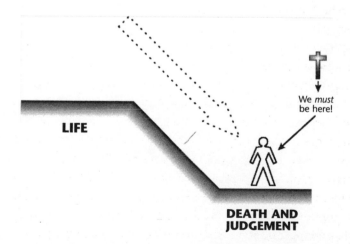

What's our situation? Where are we? Are we free to live forever? Or are we under sentence of death for our sins? I've argued in this chapter that as we look at the love of God expressed in the death of his Son on the cross, we must be under sentence of death for our sins. For some good reason, God must punish sin.

But we haven't yet looked much at what that reason might be. We know God must punish sin, but we don't yet really know why. And the one objection that we haven't yet dealt with is the one which asks about the purpose of punishing sin. What is it that's so serious about sin that God is so determined to punish it? And what does that punishment achieve? These are the questions we now move on to.

4. Real Outrage

THE CHANCES ARE, WE STILL SIMPLY DON'T GET IT. Just what is it that's so serious about sin that brings God to react so powerfully against it?

We're going to spend most of the rest of the book seeking answers to that question. But even at this stage, we can to some extent see that it might simply be right for God to punish sin. There is such a thing as *real outrage*. Perhaps we're not able to give a particularly lucid account of what it means for something to be 'outrageously wrong'. But it certainly *feels right* to say that wrongdoing deserves to be punished. That is, most of us can see that some sins by some people simply deserve to be punished. For many people, though not all, certain acts will seem *so outrageous* that the only punishment which feels appropriate is death.

The man who deserved to die
There's a very striking biblical example of this from the life of

King David, recorded in chapter 12 of the Old Testament book of 2 Samuel. There has been a catastrophic incident in David's life. God sends the prophet Nathan to him. And Nathan tells a story...

> And the LORD sent Nathan to David. He came to him and said to him: 'There were two men in a certain city, one rich and the other poor. The rich man had many flocks and herds, but the poor man had nothing but one little ewe lamb, which he had bought. And he brought it up, and it grew up with him and his children. It used to eat of his morsel and drink from his cup and lie in his arms, and it was like a daughter to him. Now there came a traveller to the rich man, and he was unwilling to take one of his own flock or herd to prepare for the guest who had come to him, but he took the poor man's lamb and prepared it for the man who had come to him'. **2 Samuel 12:1-4**

It's a story that could be told in any age: about the abuse of the poor by the rich. The poor man has nothing but a little lamb, which he loves dearly. The rich man is not just rich, but stinking rich—he has vast herds of cattle and sheep. But when someone comes to visit, instead of using what is his, he takes the only thing that the pauper possesses. David's reaction to the story is immediate:

> Then David's anger was greatly kindled against the man, and he said to Nathan, 'As the LORD lives, the man who has done this deserves to die, and he shall restore the lamb fourfold, because he did this thing, and because he had no pity'. **2 Samuel 12:5-6**

David burns with anger: 'As the LORD lives, the man who has done this deserves to die...'

But what is punishment for?

It's a feeling we can readily identify with. But it's a feeling you may think doesn't stand up well to close scrutiny. OK, so David burns with anger. He is convinced this man ought to be punished. More than that: he deserves to die. But what would the death of this man actually achieve? How would that make things better? Even if David's anger subsided, well, so what? When it comes down to it, is there actually any substance to the claim that someone simply 'deserves' to be punished?

'The humanitarian theory of punishment'

Most famous for his Narnia stories, the Oxford academic C S Lewis was also a strident defender of the Christian faith. He had a refreshing bluntness. It's a style that no doubt irritated many of his more sensitive contemporaries. On the other hand, it certainly makes him very quotable!

A good example of Lewis' bluntness can be found in an essay he wrote shortly after the Second World War with the title *The humanitarian theory of punishment*. Indeed, it may have been that Lewis' argument was simply too counter-cultural for the English climate at the time. He seems to have had great difficulty getting it published. It eventually came out in 1949 in Australia, where perhaps they are made of sterner stuff.

Lewis describes this modern theory like this:

> According to the Humanitarian theory, to punish a man because he deserves it, and as much as he deserves, is mere revenge, and, therefore, barbarous and immoral. It is maintained that the only legitimate motives for punishing are the desire to deter others by example or to mend the criminal. When this theory is combined, as frequently happens, with the belief that all crime is more or less pathological, the idea of mending tails off into that of healing and curing and punishment becomes therapeutic...

That argument still strikes a chord today. To punish someone 'because they deserve it' is something you will regularly find described as 'barbarous and immoral'. To have such a vengeance motive behind punishment might have its place in the comic-book violence of a Tarantino movie like *Kill Bill* (tagline: 'A roaring rampage of revenge!'), but not surely in the real world. To remove such crude motivation and focus instead on the more rational objectives of deterrence and rehabilitation is surely more civilised? Lewis comments:

> Thus it appears at first sight that we have moved from the harsh and self-righteous notion of giving the wicked their deserts to the charitable and enlightened one of tending the psychologically sick. What could be more amiable?

However, Lewis then goes on to argue that a great deal is lost by removing from our understanding of punishment the idea of giving the wicked what they deserve. He claims the Humanitarian theory breaks the link between punishment and justice. What's more, it treats the criminal as something subhuman, an object to be controlled for other ends. And it places punishment in the hands of 'experts'. For rehabilitation we must depend on the expert in social psychology. For deterrence we depend on the expert in social behaviour. All this is open to abuse, leaving us vulnerable to manipulation and, ultimately, to tyranny.

The big weakness of Lewis' essay is that he doesn't really address the issue of what it means to 'deserve punishment', and why that links punishment to justice. (Neither shall we in this chapter, although it will be the focus of the remaining chapters.) However, he is very astute in stripping away the civilised veneer from modern theories of punishment—the illusion that they are somehow more 'enlightened' than the common thoughts of ordinary people. And that's particularly so when it comes to rehabilitation.

A Clockwork Orange

We couldn't have a better picture of just what frightened Lewis about rehabilitation than the world we enter in Anthony Burgesses' novel *A Clockwork Orange*.

In many ways this is an obscene book. I don't mean by that that it should never have been written, but that it is frequently stomach-churning in its depiction of violence.

The central character, Alex, is a fifteen year-old leader of a violent gang in some future world. He and his friends indulge in random acts of aggression, including rape and murder. Alex tells his story in a teenage slang called 'Nadsat', made up from Russian words mixed with English. It's a challenge to read, but very effective at bringing us close to Alex's inner thought life and distancing us somewhat from the horror of what he's up to. It's an uncomfortable experience, especially when you pause to think about what Alex and his friends are actually doing.

But it's the depiction of the 'treatment' Alex receives from the authorities once he is caught that makes this an important book. Alex is treated with drugs as he watches films of his favourite activities. Strapped to a chair, with his eyelids forced open, he has to watch scenes of brutal violence, sexual and otherwise. The drugs he receives bring him to associate those images and ideas with profound feelings of physical sickness. He is being treated, in other words, like one of Pavlov's dogs. He is treated like 'a clockwork orange' ('a queer orange' is cockney slang for a strange person). And the treatment is effective. Alex is 'cured' to the point where he becomes sick at the mere thought of violence.

And that is rehabilitation. It means quite literally treating a person like a dog. It's rehabilitation taken to an extreme, to be sure. But why not take it to such extremes—if it works?

The interesting thing, of course, is that we have never quite found the resolve in our society to take rehabilitation to such a level. Perhaps it will be different if sophisticated gene therapies are ever developed to treat social dysfunction. We shall see. But as things stand, we're able to see how ugly it would be to treat someone like Alex. And, indeed, how dangerous it would be for the authorities to have such power. It reminds us of the worst abuses in the Soviet gulag prison system. Even in the novel, a political storm results in Alex's conditioning being removed. So we may talk about punishment as rehabilitation, but we don't really have the stomach to do it effectively. If anything, our prisons are places of dehabilitation, where the culture of criminality is reinforced, not diminished.

Deterrence: dangerous or not?

So what about deterrence? Lewis was worried that when deterrence becomes the reason why we punish, it opens the door to a whole package of potential abuses. When deterrence is the reason why we punish, the exercise of punishment is taken away from ordinary people. It is placed instead in the hands of technical experts who 'in the light of previous experiment, can tell us what is likely to deter'. What's more, when deterrence is the reason why we punish, why always punish the guilty? So long as people *think* a person is guilty, the deterrence works just as well.

Was Lewis right to be nervous about deterrence?

Well, yes and no. No, in that it would be fair to say that Lewis failed to acknowledge how widespread and important deterrence is in the way we interact socially. Yes, because despite that, deterrence remains too narrow a way to understand punishment.

What's changed in the fifty odd years since Lewis was writing is that we now have better and fuller explanations of how deterrence works in society. Punishment intended to deter is far more widespread that he thought. It's more than just a part of the civil administration of punishment. It's something we do all the time. It's part of the give and take of everyday life. We punish each other. Usually, thankfully, rather mildly. But when someone betrays our trust, we often punish them—even if it's only by a sour remark. It may not be a good thing, but co-operation in our working relationships often depends on that fear of being upset by someone. Sometimes, of course, the punishments we impose on those around us can be rather more severe.

The most sophisticated way to talk about this sort of interaction comes from a rather esoteric subject called 'Game Theory'. So-called because as we function socially, we make interactive choices rather as people do when they're playing a game. What Game Theory suggests is that when people interact over the long-term, punishment—or, at least, the credible threat of punishment—works to sustain social conventions.

In this way of thinking, the civil administration of punishment is just part of a much wider phenomenon. Under this understanding of punishment, there are good reasons why we might get the civil authorities to administer some kinds of punishment. Keeping a social convention by threatening to punish people who break it is a costly business. It can only work if we keep a very close eye on each other. However, in large societies it's simply impractical for every individual to do that. That results in a temptation to leave it to others and the danger that monitoring behaviour breaks down altogether. So we develop specialists to monitor behaviour and administer punishment:

the police and the courts. This is all part of the 'social contract' which keeps social conventions going. Or so the story goes.

There's enough credibility in these newer ways of thinking about deterrence to suggest that C. S. Lewis' fears were exaggerated. Deterrence is not just something 'experts' do, it's something we all do. Now it's true, civil authorities being what they are, that we can't rule out the possibility of people being publicly 'boiled in oil' as an example, even if they're entirely innocent and even for the least of crimes. But, thank God, there are checks and balances in even the most corrupt societies. We don't have to delve too far into history to see how unwilling we are to comply with authorities who might punish us even when we're innocent.

In any case, surely we want to uphold the truth that punishment and the threat of punishment can have good effects on people's behaviour? There's a great deal in the biblical account, for example, to show that the punishment administered by God often has an intended effect on behaviour. We can see in everyday life that deterrence is at least sometimes a good thing. And God agrees. God 'chastises' his people; he 'disciplines' them. He is like a loving father who doesn't want his children to play with fire. His people learn not to do certain things by being deterred from them.

But deterrence can't be the whole story
However, against that it has to be said that *most* of the references in the Bible to God acting in punishment do not have such a focus. His punishments may have an effect on behaviour, but broadly speaking, he punishes for other reasons—reasons we shall investigate more closely in later chapters. And we shall find that there's much more to punishment than mere deterrence.

Indeed, we only have to consider Jesus' death on the cross to see this must be true. Suppose the purpose of divine punishment was only to serve the future good of society by providing a deterrent against sin. Why then would God punish his only Son on the cross? In this view, the punishment taken by his Son would be no more than a particularly graphic example of what God will do to sinners. It would be intended to change our behaviour and no more. But does God depend on our behaviour that much? So much that he sends his own Son as an example? There must be more to it than that!

So where have we got to? We've seen that the feeling we all have to some extent or other that it's right to give the wicked what they deserve is a real feeling, an authentic response to wrong-doing. We've seen that in King David. We've also begun to wonder what it means, what substance it has to it. But when we take away the idea of giving the wicked what they deserve from our understanding of punishment, what we're left with doesn't seem to have much substance to it either. Certainly not enough to be the last word. And, anyway, the idea stubbornly refuses to die. You only have to open a newspaper to see that.

Crimes that cry out for justice

I read the *Daily Mail* today. Oh boy! The *Daily Mail* is a British newspaper with a certain reputation for campaigning rather vigorously for what it would call 'traditional values'. Actually, to be fair, most of what I read today was fairly mundane—not very different from what you might find in similar newspapers. But every once in a while there would be a report or a columnist who (despite reading in my head) would make my ears ache. Maybe you read the *Mail* every day, or even write for it! In which case, please forgive my insensitivity. Or maybe you're turned off by the harsh tone of tabloid columnists, in which case you'll understand my reaction.

I guess we get the press we deserve in the same way that we get the politicians we deserve. We like to have our opinions supported and reinforced—or, at least, not challenged too much. Our press reflects what we're like—warts and all. And the *Mail* assures us that many of us think certain criminals simply deserve to die.

Take Simon Heffer, writing the day after a young man called Ian Huntley was found guilty of murdering two ten year-old girls in horrifying circumstances. The article had the title: *Why I'd gladly hang Huntley*. This was the heart of it:

> Not only is it hard to keep sentimentality and emotion out of a case such as this, it is utterly wrong. Our law is founded, or should be founded, on justice. And justice means doing what human beings, emotional and sentimental as they may be, believe to be right. ...[It] is a question of what the appropriate punishment is. ... I do not support the death penalty for all murders. But for a crime as bestial and calculated as this, where a young man has murdered two small girls for what can only be construed as his own gratification, anything less than Huntley paying with his own life is singularly inappropriate.

And you can see what Simon Heffer means by justice: '...justice means doing what human beings, emotional and sentimental as they may be, believe to be right'. Many people will find that almost laughably simplistic. But he's factually correct on one thing. When it comes to the particularly horrific crimes which come to dominate our news from time to time, it is the death penalty that a great many people believe to be right.

This isn't the place to discuss the rights and wrongs of the death penalty. However, whatever you think of the *Mail*, you'll be aware to some extent of the emotion behind such expressions of outrage. I was once foolish enough to read in full a newspaper account describing in detail the death of one of the daughters of Fred and Rosemary West. To murder one's own daughter is obscene enough, but to murder her like that... Apparently, they then buried her in the garden under the Wendy House. It literally made me feel sick. I didn't need any special conditioning to feel sick. It was quite natural.

Or think of the photographs taken on the liberation of Belsen, now part of the archive of the Imperial War Museum. The concentration camp of Bergen-Belsen in Germany was liberated by British forces in April 1945. They found *sixty thousand prisoners*, most of them seriously ill. The photographs show hundreds of corpses lying unburied on the camp grounds. More than 10,000 former prisoners died after the liberation, too ill to recover. There are photographs of the mass graves, casually filled with some 50,000 bodies.

Take the most 'enlightened' and liberal-minded person on the issue of punishment you can find and show them those photographs. I would be surprised if there was no response of outrage. There would almost certainly be a feeling of disgust—not just at the crime itself, but also at those responsible. What's more, it would be a feeling quite separable from any wider thoughts of deterring something like Belsen from happening again (although that would obviously also be a good thing to strive for). And a feeling certainly quite distant from any desire to 'rehabilitate' the people who committed such crimes.

As C. S. Lewis noted, it's a feeling which most modern theories of punishment want to do away with. But it doesn't take much delving into contemporary culture, or our own experience, to see that it's something that stubbornly refuses to die.

Who deserves to be punished?

But let's return to the account we began this chapter with. The account of the prophet Nathan's encounter with King David, and the story of the rich man feasting on the poor man's beloved lamb. Nathan doesn't need to outline a sophisticated theory of punishment to make the injustice clear. It's obvious. David burns with anger and says to Nathan, 'As the LORD lives, the man who has done this deserves to die...'

But then comes Nathan's devastating twist. We can imagine him looking David right in the eye. Slowly, surely, deliberately, he says, 'You are the man!'

You see, the whole world knows that David has committed a series of obscene crimes. David is a rich man, far richer than anyone around him. He's even 'richer' when it comes to his relations with women. Against the commandment of God, he has assembled around himself a vast harem of wives and concubines. And yet when he sees a woman he fancies who's the wife of a poor and faithful neighbour, he simply takes her for himself. And then he arranges for her innocent husband to die in battle. The whole world can see the scandal. Except, it seems, for King David himself. But he can see it now.

And that's us through and through, isn't it? We can see injustice, for sure. But we're very bad at seeing it in ourselves.

I've said that the press often gives us a reflection of ourselves. When it comes to our outrage at terrible crimes, there it is, the same outrage staring back at us. But there's another aspect to what we see in that reflection: our own self-righteousness. That is, there's something of the *Daily Mail* in all of us. And one way of looking at the almost ghoulish obsession in the tabloid press with horrible crime is this: *It feeds our insatiable hunger to accuse anyone but ourselves.* We wallow in a steady supply of hate-figures. We feel secure in ourselves and our conduct in such company.

But what sort of standard are we using to declare that beyond doubt they deserve punishment, perhaps even death, but we do not? What makes one crime outrageous and another trifling? We (rightly) think that bad crimes should be punished more than lesser crimes, but also seem to think that means some crimes can effectively be left alone. Our crimes, in particular, that is.

In the chapters that follow, we're going to explore more deeply God's verdict on what is and isn't outrageous. What we shall find is that many acts that may seem to us relatively innocent actually have lurking behind them something much more sinister. That is, an attitude to God that insults him and puts him to one side. When our view of the world has no place for God, this may not feel very bad. But the more we admit that God is at the centre of everything, the more deserving of punishment we have to accept such acts are.

What we shall see will confirm that our feelings that wicked people simply deserve to be punished are not empty. We still have some right sense of justice. Which means we should be able to see instinctively that God must punish sin because it's right to punish wrongdoing—even when the contemporary understanding of punishment is pulling us away from that. It is right to be horrified by wrongdoing.

However, the scope of what deserves punishment will turn out to be much wider than we may have thought. Our sense of justice is clouded: it is biased and narrow. Instincts can be deceptive. In the end, we shall find that it's only through a sleight of hand, a movement of the ethical goal-posts in our own favour, that we can pardon ourselves.

5. God is Creator

WE'VE BEEN THINKING ABOUT the fact that most of us, at least some of the time, can see that some acts by some people simply deserve to be punished. As C. S. Lewis noted, that's a concept which most modern theories of punishment want to do away with. But it doesn't take much delving into contemporary culture, or our own feelings, to see that it's a concept that stubbornly refuses to die.

On the other hand, if that's no more than a feeling, it's not really a very strong foundation for insisting that God must punish sin. When it comes to the details, there is much disagreement about what does and what does not deserve punishment. Disagreement, too, about how much punishment a given act deserves. Let's face it: on these issues we're unreliable and biased.

So what we're going to do in the next three chapters is to turn to more solid ground. We're going to explore the possibility that the ground of justice lies in God himself. What does and does not deserve punishment ultimately depends on him and his character. He is Creator. He is LORD. He is good. And we start at the very beginning by turning to the account of God as Creator in the first book of the Bible, the Old Testament book of Genesis.

It's in verses 16 and 17 of chapter 2 of Genesis that we find God himself making the definitive link between sin and the punishment of death:

> And the LORD God commanded the man, saying, 'You may sure-
> ly eat of any tree in the garden, but of the tree of the knowledge
> of good and evil you shall not eat, for in the day that you eat of
> it you will surely die'. **Genesis 2:16-17**

God will certainly punish sin with death because he promised to, right back when he established the world in which we live.

Reading Genesis

Now if you're not familiar with the book of Genesis, you might find the claim here difficult to take seriously. Surely, of all the books in the Bible, is not Genesis the one the modern mind must dismiss as irrelevant and untrue—as mere myth and fantasy?

And if you read the book of Genesis in a way it was never intended to be read, you would indeed run into problems. Read as a modern text-book on cosmology, for example, it would indeed be difficult to take seriously. But then, notwithstanding reams of modern literary philosophy to the contrary, it's just common sense that you need to read things on their own terms. By which I mean, on the terms their authors intended. If you read a book on wood-carving as a cookery book, for example, you would quickly run into difficulty—terrible indi-gestion, for a start.

On the other hand, if we do take the trouble to read Genesis on its own terms, we find something extraordinary. We find something that confuses us at first because it's so different. But the more we read it, the more we realise just how carefully constructed it is. How beautifully concise it is. What an immense privilege it is to read, because it allows us to step 'outside the box' completely. It allows us to see our universe in its proper perspective.

It's only from this perspective that we can properly see the relationships at the heart of the universe. You see, the book of Genesis sets up a massively important distinction between the Creator, on the one hand, and his creation, on the other. And if we wanted to sum up the relationship between the two in one word it would be this: *dependency*. The Creator depends on no-one and nothing. Everything else depends exclusively on him. Upon this distinction everything else rests.

The generous Creator

The promise, or warning (depending on how you look at it), that God makes to the first man about the consequences of stepping 'out of bounds' is in chapter 2 of the book of Genesis. In these early chapters we see very clearly the careful construction of the book. We carefully build up to the commandment in verses 16 and 17. Then we see the turning point, when the commandment is broken. Then we see the warning of verses 16 and 17 carried out.

The background to the commandment, earlier in chapter 2, is very striking. Rules and commandments may sound to our ears restrictive and ungenerous. But no one could miss the amazing generosity of God displayed in these chapters. He takes a completely barren setting and fills it with abundant life.

Only the Creator can be that generous. Only he can take dry dusty ground, form a man, and breathe life into him. He is the one who provides the water needed for life, from springs and great rivers. He is the one who plants a garden for the man, 'pleasant to the sight and good for food'.

This is far from someone being generous at a distance, like some wealthy benefactor occasionally sending a large cheque to his protégée. This is no absentee landlord. This is no transcendent deity beyond our reach and understanding.

No, this is the LORD God, the LORD who forms close relations with his people. The detailed imagery in this part of the account shows us the intimate presence of the LORD in the midst of his people.

So that when we read here of the LORD God placing the man in the garden to work it and take care of it, we know that this is no burden for the man. With the LORD of Life intimately present, this is, to use Jesus' expression, life in all its fullness.

The Promise-Maker

So there is exceptional freedom in the garden. Freedom for every kind of good self-expression, artistic endeavour – whatever you can think of. There is only one rule:

> You may surely eat of any tree in the garden, but of the tree of
> the knowledge of good and evil you shall not eat, for in the day
> that you eat of it you will surely die.

The 'knowledge of good and evil'—it's a rather mysterious phrase. But it would seem to be a wisdom to know good and evil that's independent of anyone else. That's confirmed by what happens next and from the way the phrase is used elsewhere in these chapters, and later in the Bible. It's appropriate for the Creator; it's off-limits for everyone else. As mere creatures in God's creation, we should be depending on him to decide and declare what is good. While to eat from 'the tree of the knowledge of good and evil' is to depend on ourselves. It's a unilateral declaration of independence. Because only the Creator has the divine right to decide what is good in his creation.

Not an arbitrary promise
That last paragraph may have left you spluttering with indignation.

If you have no problem with saying that the Creator decides and declares what is good in his creation, then this section is not for you, and you may want to skip ahead. But we're going to tackle an issue that over the years has spun the heads of the cleverest of people. If you are currently of the persuasion that making an appeal to God and what he says is no help at all in deciding what is good or bad, then that's an important issue we need to clear up.

If that is you, then it may well be because of something that has become known as 'the Euthyphro dilemma' – hard to spell and even harder to pronounce! But the argument based on the Euthyphro dilemma is flawed. And that's most obvious when we go back to the original story upon which it's based. The original story comes from the philosopher Plato, writing about his hero Socrates.

Euthyphro, and his mischievous dilemma
According to Plato, as Socrates was waiting to be tried before King Archon in 399 B.C. (the trial that would eventually lead to his death), he fell into conversation with Euthyphro, one of the other waiting litigants. Euthyphro was waiting to prosecute

his own father for the murder of one of his hired hands. He claimed that what he was doing was holy because such murder was disagreeable to the gods. In response, Socrates asked him a characteristically Smart Aleck question. Socrates said: 'So, are acts holy because they're agreeable to the gods, or agreeable to the gods because they're holy?'

We can put the dilemma posed by Socrates like this:

- *Either* an act is good only because the gods approve of it, and say so—so that, for example, murder would be good if the gods said so,

- *Or* the gods approve of an act because it *is* good—in which case they are using an *external standard* that is independent and superior, and we still have not established why 'good' is good.

The Euthyphro dilemma is enough for contemporary philosophers such as Peter Singer to dismiss any idea that God is of relevance to thinking about what is right and what is wrong. Even if it were true that there's a wider context to our existence than people commonly assume, says Singer, we would essentially be in the same position of working out for ourselves what is good. Euthyphro shows that anything God might declare on goodness would either be arbitrary or be unexplained.

Platonic cosmology

However, there's something rather odd about the way the Euthyphro dilemma is framed. It rather depends upon 'the gods' being very limited creatures.

In Plato's way of thinking about the universe, that was indeed the case. If you have the stomach for such things, you can read some of Plato's accounts of creation in another of his books called the *Timaeus*. The striking thing about Plato's understanding is that 'the gods' are essentially creatures. They do some work in helping to create other things, working like subcontractors for a 'craftsman' who lurks distantly in the background. But they themselves are part of the fabric of the created universe.

Which, not surprisingly, has a huge impact on their moral authority. And we can see how easy it is for Plato's Socrates to ridicule anything they might have to say.

So take the first 'horn' of the dilemma. An act is good because the gods say so. Well, Socrates might say to Euthyphro, what if they said your father murdering his hired hand was good? Now with the universe fixed and given, with the way it fits together outside the control of the gods, of course that looks absurd. With the universe the way it is, we can see that murder could never be good.

Or take the second 'horn'. The gods approve of an act because it is good. 'Good' is then an external standard. But it's only possible to talk of a standard external to the gods because they sit in a wider context. Because they too are part of creation.

It comes down to this: The Euthyphro dilemma is understandable from the point of view of ancient Greek thought, where the gods were little more than superhuman, subject to the physical constraints of the universe in a similar way to mere morals—albeit to a lesser extent. When it comes to defining what is 'good', such creatures would be in the same position as you or me. They would have to take what is feasible in terms of relationships and behaviour as given. It is therefore unsurprising that their existence would, as Socrates rightly pointed out, leave us with the same problems pinning down what is 'good' that you or I have on our own.

Now you may have noticed a delicious irony here. The 'gods' in Plato's understanding are in the same position when it comes to declaring what is good as any other creature, including any group of human 'experts' on ethics. Like moral philosophers, for example. We could equally well run the argument like this: the Euthyphro dilemma shows that anything Peter Singer might have to declare on goodness to be either arbitrary or unexplained.

Why what God says is good, is good.

The God of the Bible, on the other hand, is the LORD, the Creator of heaven and earth. He made the heavens and the earth, indeed, out of nothing. That's strongly hinted at in Genesis chapter 1, and spelt out more explicitly elsewhere. 'All things were made through him,' says the apostle John; 'and without him was not anything made that was made'.

This means that what he says about goodness is not arbitrary. He can say with authority what is right and good because he is the one who dictates through creation how the universe fits together and relates to himself. That is, what God says is 'good' really is good because he is God and also because that is the way he made the universe.

So Socrates could not say of the God of the Bible, 'what if the LORD God said your father murdering his hired hand was good?' That is not an option because the LORD God hasn't made a universe in which murder is good. (And, we might add, it's hard even to conceive of God choosing to make a universe in which murder was good.)

What's more, Socrates couldn't respond, 'Aha, so the LORD God says murder is not good because it's "not good". And "not good" is some external standard which has nothing to do with him'. Socrates couldn't say that because what the LORD God says about goodness is not according to some unexplained, external standard. He chose to make this particular universe according to a certain standard: that's true. But it wasn't an external standard. He is the self-sufficient, independent Creator who makes the universe out of nothing. As he chose, there was nothing external to him! He chose according to his own goodness. And there was nothing constraining him from putting that into practice.

Which is why, in the account of God making the universe in Genesis chapter 1, we find the repeated refrain, 'And God saw that it was good'. And when he had finished, the declaration is this: 'And God saw everything he had made, and behold, it was very good' (verse 31).

So the 'knowledge of good and evil', the wisdom to know good and evil that's independent of anyone else, is a knowledge appropriate for the Creator alone. Only the Creator has the divine right to decide what is good in his creation. And what the good Creator says is good, is good. Including the command not to eat of the tree of the knowledge of good and evil.

Stepping over the boundary

So the command in the garden is not to eat of the tree of the knowledge of good and evil. We've already seen that when God talks here about 'knowing good and evil' he means much more than knowing the difference between right and wrong. He's talking about the authority to decide and declare what's right and wrong. And we see that confirmed when we turn to see what happened when this command was first broken. We shall also confirm that breaking this command is doing much more that than simply stepping over an arbitrary boundary.

This is how the account of breaking the command begins:

> Now the serpent was more crafty than any other beast of the field that the LORD God had made.
>
> He said to the woman, 'Did God actually say, "You shall not eat of any tree in the garden"?'
>
> And the woman said to the serpent, 'We may eat of the fruit of the trees in the garden, but God said, "You shall not eat of the fruit that is in the midst of the garden, neither shall you touch it, lest you die" '.
>
> But the serpent said to the woman, 'You will not surely die. For God knows that when you eat of it your eyes will be opened, and you will be like God, knowing good and evil'. **Genesis 3:1-5**

Believing the lie

We're not told very much about the serpent here, except that he's 'crafty'. And he's clearly a liar against God (which is what links him to the figure called 'Satan' later in the Bible). And the lie he tells here is a particularly blatant contradiction of what God has said. He says to the woman, 'You will not surely die'.

We may note that anyone who similarly denies that the just punishment for rebellion against God is death places themselves firmly on the side of the serpent.

Notice also how first the women and then the man become complicit in this lie. The first characteristic of stepping over the boundary set by God is *unbelief*. Rather than believe what her LORD and Creator said, the woman believes the serpent.

The sin

Then, once the lie has been believed, the unbelief of the man and woman in God begins to express itself in other ways. There's an ungrateful lack of contentment. They have been given life in all its fullness, yet they desire and covet the one thing they're denied. (Rightly denied, as we have noted—it can *only* belong to God.)

Then there's revolt and rebellion. It's the exclusive right of the LORD God, the good Creator who knows his creation, to declare what is good and evil. But when the serpent says *'you will be like God'*, the woman makes up her mind to take the fruit, and so does the man.

Finally, there's simple disobedience. There's one command in the garden, one boundary marker, and the man and woman break it.

Unbelief, discontentment, rebellion, disobedience. These are the ugly characteristics of what's called 'sin' later in the Bible. This is what God promises to punish.

The sentence executed

We've argued that the command not to eat of the tree of the knowledge of good and evil is an entirely appropriate rule. It's entirely appropriate given the distinction we've seen in the book of Genesis between Creator and creation. But we still may be wondering whether the threat to punish sin with death is credible. Will God really act on what he's said?

We issue threats all the time: some credible, some not. I often rather hastily issue threats in difficult situations that I immediately wish I hadn't. Like getting a coat on one of my five year-old children in that traumatic ten minutes before they're due to leave for school. Now that's difficult, and I'm often rather stupidly threatening to leave them behind or whatever. Threats like that frequently go wrong of course: children soon get wise to when you must be bluffing.

But was God making a promise he had no intention of keeping? Was God bluffing when he made this promise?

I think we've seen enough to see that's unlikely. The LORD God responds decisively. This is how he addresses Adam:

> 'Because you have listened to the voice of your wife and have eaten of the tree of which I commanded you, "You shall not eat of it", cursed is the ground because of you; in pain you shall eat of it all the days of your life; thorns and thistles it shall bring forth for you; and you shall eat the plants of the field. By the sweat of your face you shall eat bread, till you return to the ground, for out of it you were taken; for you are dust, and to dust you will return.' **Genesis 3:17-19**

Life will be hard, and then he will die, returning from the dry ground he was created from.

The man and the woman are excluded from the life-giving presence of God that very day. They don't physically die that day: God mercifully delays the final execution. But, effectively, they die that very day. From that moment they are what the apostle Paul calls 'dead in their trespasses'. And far from finding the 'freedom' to be like God , they find themselves in slavery. Not least of which is a slavery to their own sin. Addicted to it. Trapped by it. In bondage to something that inevitably, inescapably and rightly leads to death. It would seem that God was not bluffing.

The Truman Show

It may not yet have become a classic, but *The Truman Show* is a film based on a sizzling idea. Released in 1998, it's about a soap-opera with a difference. Truman Burbank has grown up thinking he lives in the idyllic island town of Seahaven. But actually, his whole world in every detail is a part of a giant TV studio set. A enormous dome has an inside surface that creates the illusion of a sky. Everything we take for granted, the wind, the rain, the night, the moon, the stars, even the sun is a high-tech special effect. Truman's wife, his mother, his best friend, the people walking down the street and working in the offices are all paid actors designed to make his world seem real. The show is put together by its creator, a man called simply and significantly Christof, from live video fed from some 5000 cameras placed around the town. They follow Truman's life 24 hours a day, seven days a week.

And the drama of *The Truman Show* is how Truman slowly but surely realises where he is. You can't keep a deceit like that going forever. And Truman is beginning to see signs of something odd. What's more, there are people on the outside campaigning for him to be released. Once in a while they beat the system and get close enough to say something to him.

The film ends with Truman standing by a door, having finally found the edge of the set. The booming voice of Christof comes seemingly from the clouds. He's now desperate that he's going to lose his star. 'Who are you?' asks Truman. 'I am the creator...' says Christof, adding quickly '...of a television show that gives hope and joy and inspiration to millions'. Christof implores Truman to stay. But Truman goes through that door. There are reports that when the film was first shown in cinemas, audiences would burst into spontaneous applause at this point.

Now you can look at this film in many ways. Is it perhaps a sort of parable against capitalism? An exposé of the manipulation and deceit of a world created around us by the marketers and advertisers? Some have said so. However, there are many hints that the film is pushing a bigger idea. It's a conflict between Truman and the 'creator' of his character, Christof, with deliberate allusions to the Genesis account. It's about Truman escaping from bondage, exchanging the constraints of a managed world for a world of freedom. Is it trying to link that with escaping from the constraints imposed on us by God? Perhaps—although admittedly the hints are quite subtle, and I guess most people watch the film without noticing them at all. But in that the hints are there, it's gently pushing an idea pushed much more clumsily in films like *Pleasantville* and *Chocolat*. At it's most crude the message sounds suspiciously like that of the serpent in Genesis chapter 3: 'Break free from all that nice but heavily-controlled mundanity; come and taste some real life!' If there were such a thing as a pro-Adam cult, this would be the sort of propaganda they might produce.

But the analogy doesn't work. The world in which Truman lived was an artificial world within our world. It depended on our world; it was made from our world... And the director was just an ordinary man. Indeed, a rather manipulative, exploitative man, who deceived Truman, and was dependent on the profits from product-placement in a show that is frankly voyeuristic. Truman's desire for freedom is a just and right desire. Christof the director has no rights over him, and has indeed greatly wronged him.

To make the analogy closer we would have to imagine that moment as Truman decides to leave the set rather differently. We would have to imagine that door leading to absolutely nowhere. A place with, well, nothing. No chance of life. And if not immediate death, some sort of slow slavery leading to death. No freedom of any meaningful sort. Such that passing through that door would be no more than suicidal.

And we would have to make the 'set' of *The Truman Show* rather different too. Not made out of the world for the world.

Just, well, made. That and nothing else. Not a place of manipulation and deceit. But a place where the Creator showers good gifts, not because he depends on it for a living, but out of sheer unadulterated generosity. Such that the choice would be between the freedom of life in all its fullness, and death. All that would make Truman's choice like Adam's. And Adam chose death.

From Adam to us

So that was Adam. That was back then. What has that got to do with us now? Well, the account of what happened in the garden sets a pattern for every relationship that follows. That is, Adam is clearly shown to us as a representative man. What's more, what happened in the garden is a representative example of what is called 'sin' later in the Bible.

It's true that we weren't there when God declared to Adam the command not to eat of the tree of the knowledge of good and evil. It's also true that we express our sin in ways that may have nothing at all to do with trees and serpents. But we live in the same creation. So the relation between sin and punishment, between sin and death, still applies to us. The apostle Paul puts it like this:

> ...sin came into the world through one man, and death through
> sin, so death spread to all men because all sinned. **Romans 5:12**

That is, the relation between sin and death was declared to Adam; it was applied to Adam when he sinned. There's much we could say about Paul's argument in chapter 5 of his letter to the Romans, but let's keep it to this one key point: Because we're in the same creation, and because of our relationship to Adam who is the representative human in that creation, *the relationship between sin and death applies to us too.*

We hate talking about death, of course—it's the great taboo of our age. But let's face it: we're all shuffling along in that long and winding queue to the grave. You can exercise like an Olympic athlete. You can control your diet with scientific precision. You can be obsessively safety-conscious. Perhaps you might move back a few places in the queue. But you can't leave it. The rebellion against God that infects us all leads to punishment by death. And the credibility of that promise is confirmed every time someone dies, which happens twice every second. Conclusive evidence that God will certainly punish your sin with death—just as he promised to, right back when he established the world in which we live.

Summary

We've actually seen two arguments in this chapter, which we can add to the picture we began to draw in the chapter *God is love:*

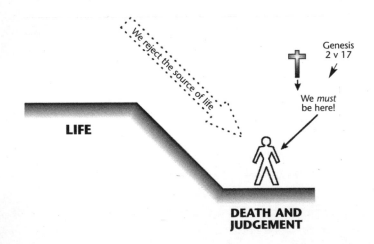

The first of the two arguments is simply that God promises to punish sin with death. The promises of God are not to be taken lightly. Just as we saw in the chapter *God is love* that as we look at the death of Jesus we know God must punish sin, so here. We know God must punish sin because he solemnly promises to.

But as we've looked at that promise in its original context, we've also been able to see more. In the context of God as Creator, with us as his dependent creatures, we've begun to see why that promise is entirely appropriate. And as we've seen more about what sin really is, the picture has become clear. As we sin, as we declare our independence from our Creator, we reject the source of life.

6. God is LORD

WE SPENT SOME TIME in the previous chapter looking at what 'sin' actually is, and why death is an appropriate outcome. In this chapter, we're going to pick up on one aspect of that: the fact that sin is about trying to wipe God out of the picture. Or, to put it another way, the fact that sin is a lie. It's a slander. It declares God not to be, when emphatically he is. It earnestly wishes him not be God. It is, as we shall see, a defamation of his 'name'.

We saw in the chapter on *Real Outrage* that punishment is not something we feel comfortable about today, and people openly wonder about what it's for. If you were to ask a competent social scientist what punishment is for, he or she might say, 'punishment functions to maintain certain social conventions, by deterring people from deviating from them'. Most people seem to think that punishment is all about rehabilitation. Either way, the modern consensus seems to be that punishment is only useful for changing people's behaviour. Any purpose for punishment beyond this seems barbaric, especially talk of God punishing.

However, if sin is a slander, a lie, a defamation of God's 'name', then punishment can be seen a different way. Rather than necessarily *changing* something (such as behaviour), it *demonstrates* something. **It demonstrates who God is.** It refutes the lies against God; it clears his name. We cannot simply do as we please, knowing that the possibility of the true ruler of the world doing anything about it is too remote to matter. God will punish rebellion, and one purpose of punishing rebellion is to demonstrate his right, just and authoritative rule.

A little later, we're going to look at some significant turning points in the biblical history of the nation of Israel. And what we shall find is that when God acts in punishment on those occasions, he clearly states his reason for doing so. It is to demonstrate and assert his status as God. He does it so that people 'may know that he is the LORD.' What's more, we shall find this determination to demonstrate who he is and what he is like at the biggest turning point of them all: the death of Jesus Christ on the cross. But first, it will help to develop a little what it means to say that sin is lie.

Sin as lie and slander

The claim here is that sin is an assault on God's authority as Creator: it's a disbelief in his justice, and a defamation of his 'name'. So when we rebel against God, it's as if we shout out a great lie: we try to say that God is not God, that he doesn't rule the world.

Now in some cases that's very obvious. If I say, 'There is no God', when there is, then that's an obvious lie. What's more, it's a *culpable* lie. When, in the Psalms of the Old Testament, King

David says, 'The fool says in his heart, "There is no God" '
(Psalm 14), he is not talking about mere ignorance. We read on
to discover that he's talking about those who are corrupt and do
no good. Similarly, if I religiously devote myself to a 'god' other
than the true God, I'm saying about the true God: 'You are not
God'. It's an obvious lie.

For some other sins need a little further though to see how
they're telling lies about God. If I murder someone, for example, what am I saying by that? I'm saying that it's me who has
rights over their life, not God (who is the source and ground of
life). Which is a lie. If I commit adultery, what am I saying by
that? I'm saying that it's me who decides on the pattern by
which men relate to women, not God (who made a world consistent with his own goodness to work a certain way). Which is
a lie. And so on.

Indeed, we don't need to dig very deep beneath any sinful act
to find the lie about God. Even 'little' sins. Suppose, for example, I exaggerate my success as a fisherman. I talk about the
three-pound trout that nearly got away but which I landed in
the end. (When, in fact the sad truth is that in all my attempts
at fishing so far, I haven't caught a thing.) I exaggerate. Surely,
that's not so serious? A bit childish, perhaps. A 'misde-
meanour', surely, not a sin?

Well, it may not seem serious, but what am I saying about
God? What would it take to make this 'exaggeration' not matter?
That God's not quite 'big' enough to notice? That his standards
are pure, maybe, but not so pure as to care about this? Or that
my own reputation is more important than the truth. These are
serious lies. And there's a serious lie beneath every sinful act.

We saw in the last chapter that the trigger for sin is believing a lie about God. Well, when we believe the lie, and then commit the sin, we become caught up in it. We join the ranks of the liars.

But what about sin as a *defamation* of God's 'name'?

Sin as defamation of God's 'name'

In the Old Testament book of Exodus, the God and Creator of the universe does an amazing thing. He introduces himself. He tells his servant Moses his name. When Moses is first confronted by God, this is what happened:

> Then Moses said to God, 'If I come to the people of Israel and say to them, "The God of your fathers has sent me to you", and they ask me, "What is his name?" what shall I say to them?' God said to Moses, 'I AM WHO I AM.' And he said, 'Say this to the people of Israel, "I AM has sent me to you." ' God also said to Moses, 'Say this to the people of Israel, "The LORD, the God of your fathers, the God of Abraham, the God of Isaac, and the God of Jacob, has sent me to you". This is my name forever, and thus I am to be remembered throughout all generations...' **Exodus 3:13-15**

It's clear that in giving his 'name', God is doing much more than giving a label to address him by. He's initiating a relationship. Which is something we might do when giving our name to someone, in introducing ourselves to them. But when God gives his name, it's also clear that he's signifying what sort of relationship that is to be. His name signifies his character, his status. His name is 'Yahweh' or, as it appears in our Bibles, 'the LORD'. The Hebrew for 'the LORD' looks a bit like the Hebrew for 'I am'. And you can see that God connects the two, telling Moses to say, 'I AM has sent me to you; ... the LORD... has sent me to you'. His name signifies that he is.

Now you may think that's more than a little enigmatic. In the context, God seems to be assuring Moses that he is, and will be for Moses the promise-keeping God he was for Abraham, Isaac and Jacob. So his name signifies his constancy and faithfulness. It's a characteristic we can trace back to the self-sufficiency, the independence, he has as Creator.

Elsewhere in scripture, we find that his name signifies that he is alive and ethically pure. He is the one in charge of history, the one who calls together a people for himself.

Later in the book of Exodus, the LORD gives Moses an even deeper insight into his character. This is what he says on that occasion:

> The LORD descended in the cloud and stood with him there, and proclaimed the name of the LORD. The LORD passed before him and proclaimed, 'The LORD, the LORD, a God merciful and gracious, slow to anger and abounding in steadfast love and faithfulness, keeping steadfast love for thousands, forgiving iniquity and transgression and sin, but who will by no means clear the guilty...' **Exodus 34:5-7a**

His name also signifies his compassion and love. And, indeed, his justice. Deny any of these truths about God and you are defaming his name.

So that's what God means by his 'name'. It's a somewhat unusual way of talking about his character and status. We still sometimes talk about someone 'making a name for themselves'. And it's language that when we use it of people rightly makes us cringe. Such open social climbing, such overt attention-seeking, is hardly commendable. Why should one ordinary human being deserve more respect and adoration than another? Nothing can add to the fact that, when it comes down to it, they are just a human. Whoever they are, and whatever they've done.

So to make a 'name' for myself is to puff up my self-importance way beyond what is defendable. I might rightly want to defend my 'name' if someone were to slander me. But there's no great reason why I should seek a 'name' that exalts me above anyone else. Which is perhaps why we don't use such language so much any more—although we still do the attention-seeking of course!

On the other hand, it is eminently appropriate language for God to use of himself. When we compare the Creator to us his creatures, there is an obvious and defendable difference in status. God doesn't need to make a name for himself. His status already gives him a 'name' that is higher than any other. So when God's name is defamed, that's doubly offensive. But the sheer 'highness' of God's name makes defaming it much, much more serious.

Joe Bloggs, liar and slanderer

To sin is to lie about God, to defame his name. We say, 'God is not God'. But of course God is God. And what we're hoping to establish in this chapter is this: *That one of the key purposes of God acting in punishment against sin is to refute each of those lies, to demonstrate who he is.*

It makes sense. But we may still be struggling to see just how deserving of punishment such slander is. So think about something similar happening to you.

Suppose you come home one evening and find that the key to your house doesn't work. You try again and again. The key bends in the lock. Then you notice evidence of someone having done some work on the door. You don't believe it – it seems someone has changed the locks! You bang on the door but there's no response. You notice a window open. With some difficulty, you break into your own house. Inside, it's quite appar-

---

* I'm sorry if your name really is Joe Bloggs, by the way—I don't mean to get at you. I imagine life must be hard enough as it is!

ent that someone else has moved in. And on every item in your house they have stamped their name in red letters. Let's call him Joe Bloggs*. So there it is. On your TV, in red security pen down the side: Joe Bloggs. On your fridge: Joe Bloggs. His name is on every thing in every room. You still can't believe it. You look inside one of your books and your name has been has been covered by a little sticker that reads, 'This book belongs to...'—and in the blank space: Joe Bloggs. Thousands and thousands of lies written all over your house and possessions. These do not belong to Joe Bloggs. Whoever he is.

Bewildered, you collapse into your desk chair. The movement prompts your computer back into life. As the screen warms up, you see a document open. It's a half-written article about you for a local newspaper. Hastily, you read through it. It's also full of lies. Slanderous, obscene accusations; and finally the writer denies that you exist at all.

What more could there be? Your eye falls on the filing cabinet. With a sigh you open a drawer. You look into your affairs, and find that the ownership deeds to your house have been changed to read, yes, Joe Bloggs; and that Joe Bloggs has found some way of accessing your bank account and your savings.

If you are anything like me, it wouldn't take long before your bewilderment turned to anger. How dare they! But after seeing red for a while, your overwhelming desire would be to set things right. You'd want to reclaim all that was rightfully yours; and to clear your name in the courts. You'd want retractions published in the newspapers. You'd want some justice to be shown. And I imagine you wouldn't be satisfied with just getting *some* of your stuff back. You wouldn't be satisfied with a partial retraction... You would want to set everything straight, wouldn't you?

It's a nightmare scenario. And it may have given you some insight into what it would be like on the receiving end of such slander and defamation. However, even if you are beginning to see that, remember that it would have been but the tiniest glimpse of the sort of injustice we're talking about in this chapter. The sort of slander and defamation we're talking here about is directed at the LORD God. It's not something one could take to the civil courts and hope to have cleared. It's a slander directed at the very ground and foundation of justice himself. If I can see how bad it would be if my personal reputation were being ground into the dust, I should be able to see how much more serious our defamation of God is.

So as we turn to look at some significant turning points in the biblical history of the nation of Israel, it should no longer come as *such* a surprise that God is determined to demonstrate and assert his status against every lie to the contrary.

The Exodus

Many years before Moses' first encounter with the LORD, the LORD God made a promise to a man called Abraham. He promised Abraham numerous descendants who would receive great blessing in a land of their own. By Moses' time, there are numerous descendents alright, millions of them. But as part of the LORD's plan, they've ended up, not in a land of their own, but in Egypt. That was fine to start with, but there's been a change of management. The current king of Egypt, or 'Pharaoh', hates the Hebrews and has reduced them to slaves. And as the cry comes up from his people, the LORD shows his determination to make good on the promise he made.

Now just before the LORD begins to intervene, he gives a very concise summary of what he's going to do and why he's going to do it. It's always handy when people do that. When I was a student, it was always something of a relief when articles you had been set to read were headed by a clear summary. Two minutes work, and there was another one to stick in the bibliography!

Let me be clear: these few verses aren't here so we don't have to read the rest of the story! They're here to give us an overview and show us the roles taken by the main characters. And the interesting thing is that the people we might expect to be important characters (that's Moses and Aaron) turn out to be rather unimportant: Just two old men with a messenger's job to do. Because, of course, the real hero in this unfolding history is the LORD God himself.

This is what the LORD God says to Moses:

> You shall speak all that I command you, and your brother Aaron shall tell Pharaoh to let the people of Israel go out of the land. But I will harden Pharaoh's heart, and though I multiply my signs and wonders in Egypt, Pharaoh will not listen to you. Then I will lay my hand on Egypt and bring my hosts, my people the children of Israel, out of the land of Egypt by great acts of judgment. The Egyptians shall know that I am the LORD, when I stretch out my hand against Egypt and bring out the people of Israel from among them. **Exodus 7:2-5**

And it quickly becomes clear as we read this account that the LORD God has a quite exceptional degree of control over what's going to happen. He makes the message he gives Moses and Aaron a powerful one. There's no doubt that when Moses and Aaron deliver the message that Pharaoh will eventually let the Hebrews go. And God, therefore, will certainly achieve the result he wants, which is the rescue of his people.

He is LORD even over the response to his message. Pharaoh's initially negative response is part of the plot. Pharaoh's slow response allows God to multiply his 'miraculous signs and wonders'. And as Pharaoh continues to dither, this paves the way for God to, 'lay his hand' on Egypt with 'great acts of judgment'. And what's the purpose of all this? Well, when all that is done:

> The Egyptians shall know that I am the LORD, when I stretch out my hand against Egypt and bring out the people of Israel from among them. **Exodus 7:5**

The Egyptians are a people who fail to acknowledge who God is, led by a Pharaoh who fails to acknowledge who God is. And because they do not acknowledge the LORD, they stubbornly refuse to let his people go. What follows from the LORD is punishment—he brings the ten plagues upon Egypt. These are destructive 'wonders' of increasing intensity. Each should be enough to show Pharaoh who he is dealing with. Each time he fails to respond properly. Until the final plague, when all the firstborn sons of Egypt are struck dead. Then Pharaoh let's God's people go. That's enough. That's enough, says God; at that point 'the Egyptians shall know that I am the LORD'.

And indeed that's a repeated refrain in the chapters that follow. We're told a little later that God is doing this to show that there is no one like the LORD. He lets Pharaoh live as witness to his power; he does it so that his name may be proclaimed in all the earth. The punishments demonstrate to Pharaoh that the earth is the LORD's. (They also demonstrate to the Israelites that the LORD is their God.) The final climatic striking down of the firstborn of Egypt is described as executing judgements on all the gods of Egypt. Again, the declaration is 'I am the LORD'. So that they know he is the LORD

And it's a repeated refrain throughout the Bible. When we turn to the next major turning point in the history of Israel, it's there over and over again. This is when the LORD acts in punishment against Israel herself. He's responding to extreme unfaithfulness from Israel, which has once again defamed his name. It's particularly striking in the book associated with the Old Testament prophet Ezekiel. Take this from chapter 5 of the book:

> Thus shall my anger spend itself, and I will vent my fury upon them and satisfy myself. And they shall know that I am the LORD – that I have spoken in my jealousy – when I spend my fury upon them. **Ezekiel 5:13**

This passage raises and answers an important question. If the LORD God is angry at the universal sin of mankind, what is it that will finally satisfy him? He will be satisfied when he has clearly demonstrated that he is the LORD.

In the next chapter of Ezekiel, why does God tear down the idols the people of Israel have been worshiping? – the idols that lie about the true God?

> Wherever you dwell, the cities shall be waste and the high places ruined, so that your altars will be waste and ruined, your idols broken and destroyed, your incense altars cut down, and your works wiped out. And the slain shall fall in your midst, and you shall know that I am the LORD. **Ezekiel 6:6-7**

Why does he do it? So that they shall know he is the LORD. And so it goes on, over and over again.

God is God. He is the Creator. He is 'the LORD'. He is merciful, yes, amazingly merciful. But not to the exclusion of his justice. And he's determined to show it. He's determined to demonstrate his authority and justice by punishing rebellion. He's determined to clear his name.

The triumph of true kings

Sellar and Yeatman's classic comedy history of England, *1066 and all That*, conveniently divides kings into three classes: Bad Kings, Good Kings and Weak Kings. Of the three, it's the Weak Kings that receive the greatest derision. King Stephen, who followed Henry I (in case you had forgotten!), was a classic Weak King, notoriously letting his Barons get away with almost anything. According to *1066 and All That* he spent much of his time arguing with his Aunt Matilda, who was claiming to be the real King. They spent the reign 'escaping from each other over the snow in nightgowns'.

So Weak Kings are a Bad Thing?

I wonder what it must have been like under, say, King Stephen, with the country in a state that more reputable historians describe as 'anarchy'? There could have been no recourse to the law, no appeal to authority. A Baron in those days could do as he pleased, knowing that the possibility of the King doing anything about it was too remote to matter. 'What King?' he might have said; '—there is no King '...

Were we to be living in such an age, I don't suppose we would have such a problem with the idea of a ruler re-establishing his rightful rule. We would be quick to support a legitimate king crushing an illegitimate rebellion. If some people were unjustly saying he wasn't rightfully king, we would understand him wanting to do something about it. Indeed, we would probably welcome the end to anarchy and uncertainty.

We no longer live in the age of kings, of course. But we don't have to travel far to see the ever-present horror of anarchy in the world. And talk of kings re-establishing rule and order is not so hard to understand that we can't see the similarities when God acts decisively to demonstrate his rightful rule. The difference being, of course, that God has far more right to be called LORD than any human king. He is the Creator, after all.

The triumph of the true King

So while the age of the rule of kings may be dead, the language of kings and kingdoms isn't so utterly unfamiliar that we can't understand it. Which is just as well, because it's the language used extensively in the New Testament to describe God re-establishing his rightful rule in Jesus Christ.

But if God is God, isn't he always 'king'? Well, yes—as the Creator, there is a sense in which God is always king. He is incontestably king over all he has created. However, there's also a sense in which that kingship is not properly expressed when the world is full of people who don't accept it. God rules, yes. But he does not rule unopposed.

So the great drama of biblical history is how God deals with that situation. How he brings in his unopposed rule. How he brings in his kingdom. Crushing the rebellion. Drawing to himself new subjects, and a new people. And we come to the final, decisive turning point in that drama with the visitation of God in the flesh—the arrival of Jesus Christ as God's King.

We read in Matthew's gospel that when Jesus began his ministry, he claimed to be the great, divine King promised by the prophets. He was bringing great light into a world of darkness. And his command was: 'Repent, for the kingdom of heaven is at hand'.

And he demonstrates, against appearances, that he truly is God's King through his death and resurrection. Once that has happened, Matthew's gospel ends with Jesus saying, 'All authority in heaven and on earth has been given to me'.

So the King is in place. But there is also a sense in which his kingdom *is still coming*. It expands as his followers turn rebels into more followers, as they take to all the nations his message to surrender to his worldwide rule. And it's a process with a clear end, a clear climax. Because there will come a point in the future when the rebellion is finally crushed forever.

The King is calling together subjects faithful to him and his cause. And the very next thing on the agenda is to bring in his unopposed rule with perfect justice. The question we all face is this: when that justice comes, will we be at the receiving end of it? Or will we be taking refuge in him?

Let's draw together the threads in this chapter so far. As sinners, we are rebels—rebelling against the rule of God. As sinners we are liars—each time we sin we utter the lie that God is not God. As sinners, we are slanderers—we rub the name of God in the dirt. But God warns us that he is determined to deal with this intolerable situation. He is determined to clear his name, to refute the lies and to re-establish his rightful, unopposed rule. And we see him doing just that as he acts in punishment throughout biblical history. Ultimately, though, he is doing it through Jesus Christ, to whom he has given all authority in heaven and on earth. Ultimately, it is Jesus Christ who will crush the rebellion.

Confirmation in the rescue

Even if you would describe yourself as a Christian, you may have found yourself having to cope with a number of new ideas in this chapter. The idea of sin being a lie, and in particular a lie about God's rule, may not be a familiar one. But I hope that this way of looking at sin has given you some insight into why God is so determined to demonstrate that he is rightly LORD of all. He is determined to demonstrate his authority and justice. Some insight, also, into why God will not be satisfied until he has dealt with every one of those lies our rebellion has levelled at him. And some insight into why we find the language of kings and kingdoms used to speak of God re-establishing his rightful rule through Jesus Christ.

But there's a very serious loose end to deal with. If all this is true, then how could God ever 'pass over' sins? How could he ever *not* deal with them directly? Because the amazing claim of the gospel is that this is exactly what he does.

At the Exodus

We've seen this 'problem' already in the book of Exodus. God is determined to bring his people out of Egypt; and he does rescue them, and even, to some extent, lives among them. But it's not that his people don't sin against him. It soon becomes apparent that in many ways his people are just as stubborn as Pharaoh. They're discontent; they're rebellious; they're unbelieving. The lies coming from them about God turn out to be as offensive as those that came from the Egyptians. And yet somehow, as he rescued them, he passed over their sins. How could that be?

Well it certainly wasn't by simply ignoring them. When the Israelites were rescued, there was special provision to allow them to avoid God's punishment. An animal had to be seen to die. The LORD was striking down dead the firstborn of Egypt. But the Israelites sprinkled animal blood round their doorposts and when the LORD saw it he passed over that house.

How did that work? Well, shed blood proclaims a death. Death, as we saw in the last chapter, is the punishment for sin. When we sin we tell a lie about God, denying that he is God. And God is only prepared to 'pass over' that if he can also demonstrate his authority and justice some other way. Either he demonstrates his authority and justice by punishing the sinner. Or he demonstrates it some other way. Some other way, by which God satisfies himself that the lies have been exposed and dealt with. At the Exodus, that was through the death of an animal. The shed blood showed he had demonstrated he is the LORD—at least partially.

On the Cross

I say that God's authority and justice were only partially demonstrated at the Exodus because of course it was only animal blood. What we discover when we get to the New Testament is this: Ultimately, to 'pass over' sins, God must demonstrate his authority and justice through the blood of Jesus. That is, through the *death* of Jesus—death being the appropriate punishment for a rebel and a liar against God.

This is how the apostle Paul puts it in the third chapter of his letter to the Christians in Rome. All have sinned against God, says Paul. But those who have faith in Jesus have the penalty of death removed. This is a gift, says Paul...

> ...through the redemption that is in Christ Jesus, whom God put forward as a propitiation by his blood, to be received by faith. This was to show God's righteousness, because in his divine forbearance he had passed over former sins. It was to show his righteousness at the present time, so that he might be just and the justifier of the one who has faith in Jesus. **Romans 3:25-26**

So God put forward Christ Jesus as a propitiation. As we saw in the chapter *God is Love*, this means a sacrifice, a death, that satisfies his justice. And why did he do that?

> ...This was to show God's righteousness, because in his divine forbearance he had passed over former sins. It was to show his righteousness...

When he 'passes over' someone's sin and removes the penalty of death, God's chosen way to demonstrate his authority and justice is through the blood of Jesus.

Just how determined is God?

Paul is saying that those who have faith in Jesus are delivered from the penalty of death as a gift. We shall come back to this amazing truth in the final chapter. But it's worth having this 'preview' now, because it helps us see the extent of God's determination to demonstrate his authority and justice.

Remember the argument we looked at in the chapter *God is Love?* Remember what the apostle John said about the love of God? He said it was most powerfully expressed when God sent his Son into the world to die so that we might live. We saw that God wouldn't have done that unless it were absolutely necessary. But would God have sent his Son to face a punishment-taking death if there were no need for the punishment to be taken?

We can argue something similar here. The apostle Paul has told us that a key purpose behind sending his Son to die was this: for people who have faith in Jesus, God demonstrates his authority and justice by punishing their sins in Jesus rather than punishing them. Was it absolutely necessary for him to demonstrate his authority and justice like that? It must have been. He wouldn't have sent his Son to die if it were not.

Think about other situations in which we might be determined to demonstrate something. I have a Canadian friend who is fearfully proud of her nation's prowess at ice-hockey. Imagine that something happened to stop Team Canada entering the next Hockey World Cup. They simultaneously knock each other out in practice, perhaps. (Dangerous game, ice-hockey.) But Canada would be determined to demonstrate its status as the premier ice-hockey nation, and would doubtless send a replacement team in their place.

Similarly, for people with faith in Jesus, something has happened. They no longer face the punishment for their sins that would demonstrate God's authority and justice. But Father and Son are *so determined* to demonstrate God's authority and justice that the Son takes the punishment in their place. Failure to punish sin would be a failure to demonstrate God's authority and justice.

So what about people without faith in Jesus? Must it not be true that God is equally determined to demonstrate his authority and justice? Equally determined, then, to punish their sin.

Either way, it would seem once again from the cross that God is determined to punish sin.

Summary

That really does make the case in this chapter watertight:

When we sin, when we rebel against God, we assault his authority, we disbelieve his justice, we defame his name, we wish he weren't God, we stupidly wish he were dead. We circulate a great lie, saying he is not God.

And rather as you and I would want to set things straight and clear if your name if you were slandered, so God acts to clear his name. A repeated refrain in the Bible is that God punishes so that people may know he is the LORD. He will not be satisfied until he has dealt with every one of those lies our rebellion has levelled at him. He will not be satisfied until he has demonstrated his authority and justice. And the cross proves it.

Let's add that to our summary picture of why God must punish sin:

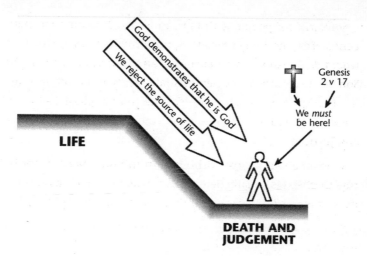

Once again, looking carefully at what happened on the cross has confirmed that we can know for sure God must punish sin. He does it because he must demonstrate his authority and justice.

Now we've already said that the punishment of death is an appropriate punishment when we suicidally reject our Creator, the very source of our life. From this chapter, we can add that the punishment of death is an entirely appropriate way for God to refute the lies and slander levelled at him by our sin. To re-establish his rule and crush the rebellion against him. To demonstrate his authority and justice. To demonstrate that he is God and LORD.

7 God is Good

WE'RE TRYING TO ESTABLISH why God must punish sin. We've seen that God is so determined not to just 'let sin go' that he was prepared to send his only Son to take the punishment in the place of people he wants to forgive. We've seen that our own intuitions, when they're working well, suggest that it is only right to punish sin. We've seen that God made a credible and meaningful promise to punish sin with death when he established the world in which we live.

And in the last chapter we looked more closely at how every act of sin is a futile act of rebellion. That is, every sin is a lie, it's something that tries to say that God is not God, that he doesn't rule the world. But of course God is God, and he uses punishment to refute each of those lies, to demonstrate who he is, to demonstrate his authority and justice.

That is, God punishes sin because God is God.

In this chapter we shall look at our final argument. The aim is to see that God punishes sin because he is good. That is, in divine punishment, God actively expresses his perfect goodness.

Talking about good and evil

We shall begin by saying this: If God is perfectly good, then, by definition, he is also perfectly opposed to that which is bad or evil or wicked. That should be uncontroversial.

However, it has to be said that people don't like talking that way about goodness. We would much prefer always to be positive. Let's suppose that all of us, in our own way, divide things into good and bad. We will usually want to express that by saying that the good things are good rather than that the bad things are bad.

And that may well be a sensitive approach in many circumstances. So that if, for example, I am judging a children's painting competition, it may not be especially kind to dwell openly on the faults of the worst paintings. Unless, that is, I actually want to be surrounded by crowds of six-year olds in tears. When I visit a friend's house, it may not be especially friendly to highlight the relative success of her living room décor by focussing on the fact that her kitchen is a mess!

But the fact remains that it becomes meaningless to express favour towards things we deem good unless we are also prepared, at least in principle, to declare our dislike of things we deem bad. Otherwise all we have is a sort of bland indifference. Where nothing is really good and nothing is really bad.

Now I need to be careful not to overstate this point. We do sometimes strongly express our dislike of things that are bad. As we noted in the chapter on *Real Outrage,* there are some things that we feel 'safe' to be outraged about. So we hear plenty of outrage about certain types of sexual abuse, about social injustice, about environmental destruction, and so on. And, for the most part, this outrage is well founded—even if it does tend to be directed at people well away from ourselves, in situations we're not too familiar with.

However, it seems to me that we're not very consistent. We seem to be rather selective about when it's good to express outrage. We don't seem to be able to associate outrage as the natural partner of declaring something good. What's your automatic reaction when I say, 'If God is perfectly good, then he is also perfectly opposed to that which is bad or evil or wicked'? Perhaps (when you've thought about it) it's a grudging: 'Well, I suppose so'. More likely that than: 'Of course he is!'

Which is a shame, because it means this: Look around at all the wickedness in the world, and the brokenness and pain that results from it. We are missing out on the assurance of knowing God is perfectly opposed to all that. Think of some of the horrific things you've heard reported in the news recently. I can guess that some military conflict is killing innocent people, breaking up communities, driving people to starvation. I can guess that there are criminal proceedings for some obscene crime against a child. I can guess that some public figure has been found lying or cheating or corrupt in some other way. Wouldn't it be good to know that God is perfectly opposed to those things?

Or think of wickedness closer to home. Imagine being the victim of some great evil yourself. Something almost too horrible even to contemplate—seeing your child murdered, perhaps. Again, wouldn't you want to know that God felt at least as strongly about that as you?

Good anger? Good hatred?

If God is perfectly good, then he is also perfectly opposed to that which is bad or evil or wicked. That should be uncontroversial. But the next step certainly is controversial, and that's to go so far as to say that **he must hate such things**; that they provoke him to anger.

That's controversial because people see the danger of importing into that some of the bad things that characterise human hatred and anger. Human anger is indeed often irrational and wicked in intent.

However, the fact remains that God uses those words of himself in the Bible. He hates sin; it provokes him to anger. In a moment, we're going to look at the temple sermon of the prophet Jeremiah. And we're going to see Jeremiah using such words as he declares the words of God. It's appropriate language. We just need to remember it's a *pure* hatred, a *pure* anger, that we're talking about.

Let's suppose I take the outrage I'm feeling about some issue in the news at the moment—or about some other issue in my life. Let's suppose I take out all the inconsistency, the selectivity, the hypocrisy. The fact that I feel angered by that, but not by something which, were I to think about it some more, I would find just as bad. Let's suppose I take out all the rough edges. Squeeze it free from bitterness and the heat of the moment. And then I multiply that feeling many, many times.

Why multiply it? Well, let's face it, I'm not perfect. The outrage I feel is tempered by my own standards of conduct—which are far from reliable. While God's outrage will be relative to a perfect standard. And I'm not the Creator. I live in the world, and therefore have some limited idea of how it works. But I don't have that intimate, exhaustive knowledge that comes from having designed and made it! A knowledge that guarantees that God gets outraged by exactly the right things. And I don't see the whole picture. While God sees evil behaviour from every perspective. Including the perspective of the victim—the people who have suffered directly from the evil, sometimes terribly. And while I will tend to be more concerned about things that are close to me and my situation, he sees and cares about all the wickedness in the world, wherever it happens.

So suppose I purify my feelings of outrage as best I can, and multiply it many, many times. If I do that, then I will then have a glimpse of what God feels about the wickedness and evil in the world. It's an outrage so perfectly intense that it's quite appropriate to call it a just and pure hatred.

But if God hates sin and evil and wickedness, that raises the following question: Can he hate those things and do nothing about them? Is there such a thing as a passive hatred of those things, something that hates at a distance but leaves it at that? Now I think the obvious answer to that is, 'No'. But let's allow God to drive that message home, as we listen to him speaking though the prophet Jeremiah.

Jeremiah's temple sermon

In chapter seven of the Old Testament book of Jeremiah, there's a sermon. It's delivered by Jeremiah at the gate of the temple about six hundred years before the birth of Christ. At least part of this chapter gives us the text of what Jeremiah actually said on that day. It's difficult to be 100% sure where the transcript ends. But the whole of the chapter, and going on into the first three verses of the next, seems to have been put together to be read out in one piece, as a whole. And it's a devastating message.

Because we'll be following Jeremiah in this section, this will be the closest we have got so far in this book to what you might call a written version of traditional 'hellfire' preaching. I say that with some hesitation, because hellfire preaching isn't exactly fashionable. It's not the sort of profession that would go down well at a posh party, is it? 'And what do you do?' someone asks over a glass of sherry. 'I'm a hellfire preacher,' you admit... There's a very long silence.

I don't want to be counter-cultural just for the sake of it, just to be annoying. However, we are hoping to get behind that sort of middle-class embarrassment to the truth about God's anger.

Jeremiah's sermon is not like many sermons you will hear today. It has more than three points for a start. There are no jokes, no humorous asides, no chit-chat. Just searing sarcasm. There are no illustrations; you can't imagine Jeremiah handing round an outline before he began, or using an OHP to project his main points. But, having said that, it's certainly isn't dull. As we shall see, Jeremiah's sermon is very graphic:

> The word that came to Jeremiah from the LORD: 'Stand in the gate of the LORD's house, and proclaim there this word, and say, Hear the word of the LORD, all you men of Judah who enter these gates to worship the LORD. Thus says the LORD of hosts, the God of Israel: Amend your ways and your deeds, and I will let you dwell in this place. Do not trust in these deceptive words: 'This is the temple of the LORD, the temple of the LORD, the temple of the LORD.' **Jeremiah 7:1-4**

The temple sermon comes at a point in the book when Jeremiah has spent chapter after chapter warning God's people of the danger they're in. These are the physical descendants of the people God brought out of slavery in Egypt. He gave them a land of their own and the temple we read about here represented his presence in their midst. But they've not lived up to this privilege. Instead, they have turned to do what is evil in the sight of God. And Jeremiah has been appealing to them to change their ways. That's an appeal he repeats here. And he adds that they must stop trusting in the temple to protect them from God's anger at what they're doing.

Trusting in the temple to cover-up wickedness is an outrageous thing to do, as we see when God's indictment against them continues like this:

> Will you steal, murder, commit adultery, swear falsely, make offerings to Baal, and go after other gods that you have not known, and then come and stand before me in this house, which is called by my name, and say, 'We are delivered!' – only to go on doing these abominations? Has this house, which is called by my name, become a den of robbers in your eyes? Behold, I myself have seen it, declares the LORD. **Jeremiah 7:9-11**

It's becoming increasingly apparent that the people have no intention of changing their ways. They will continue to deal with each other unjustly. They will continue to follow other gods to their own harm. Indeed, we find the whole family involved. Later in the chapter, we're shown a very 'homely' little scene:

> Do you not see what they are doing in the streets of Judah and in the streets of Jerusalem? The children gather wood, the fathers kindle fire, and the women knead dough, to make cakes for the queen of heaven. And they pour our drink offerings to other gods, to provoke me to anger. **Jeremiah 7:17-18**

The whole family together—how lovely! The whole family united... but united in turning away from the one true God, and worshipping 'gods' of their own making. And that's nothing compared with what's going on in the Valley of the Son of Hinnom:

> For the sons of Judah have done evil in my sight, declares the LORD. They have set up their detestable things in the house that is

> called by my name, to defile it. And they have built the high places
> of Topheth, which is in the Valley of the Son of Hinnom, to burn
> their sons and their daughters in the fire... **Jeremiah 7:30-31**

This is the sort of ritual human sacrifice that took place in the land before God gave it to the Israelites. But the practice has come back as the Kings of southern Israel, Judah, have turned to wickedness. There was a brief respite under the reforms of King Josiah. But when Josiah's son is replaced by the brother of the King of Egypt, the practice seems to have returned with a vengeance.

It's difficult to think of anything more disgusting, isn't it? To take one's son or daughter and burn them alive to god who doesn't even exist. And it's from committing such abominations that the people keep coming back to the temple of the LORD for deliverance.

But they will not be delivered. The temple is no refuge. Offerings and sacrifices will provide no protection. In the face of such unrepentant disobedience, the punishment of the LORD is sure and certain and terrifying:

> Therefore thus says the LORD God: behold, my anger and my
> wrath will be poured out on this place, upon man and beast, on
> the trees of the field and the fruit of the ground; it will burn and
> not be quenched. **Jeremiah 7:20**

In fact, the punishment poured out on Judah and Jerusalem will be so intense that the Valley of Hinnom will become the Valley of Slaughter, filled with the dead until there is no more room, their bones lying open and defiled, like bone-meal fertiliser spread out under the stars they used to worship.

We're not surprised when we learn later in the book that for saying such things Jeremiah was seized by the priests and the people, who had every intention of killing him. It seems hell-fire preaching has *never* been very popular.

Good anger, actively expressed

But do you see the pattern? The people provoke the LORD to anger. We can see why he's angry. We can see that he's right to be angry. But the LORD's anger is not a passive anger. His reaction to being so provoked is an active one. He may patiently delay his reaction, but ultimately he won't let his determination to punish go unsatisfied.

And how could it be otherwise? What a bizarre inconsistency it would be to hate something, to be able to do something about it, but then to do nothing! Imagine you visited a friend who has a phobia about spiders, and in their living room you find case after case of... tarantulas! Why doesn't he get rid of them? Or you have a rug in your hall in psychedelic colours that gives you a headache and makes you sneeze uncontrollably. Why is it still there? Why haven't you thrown it out?

But we find no such inconsistency, no such absurdity, in God. There is nothing constraining him from acting on his anger. Which gives a very close connection between God's anger and God expressing his anger in punishment. And it's not just a peculiarity of Jeremiah's temple sermon. We find it throughout the book of Jeremiah and throughout the Bible. In only a tiny handful of cases where God's anger is mentioned is there no mention of God acting upon it. Elsewhere, we're told that God clears the way for his anger to be expressed. Time and time again the imagery of fire is used to describe God's righteous anger. But this is not the 'inward fire' of the emotion of anger. No, the refrain throughout the Bible is that God is 'a consuming fire'. His anger is active, tangibly experienced by those he is angry with.

God's good anger at us

If God is perfectly good, then he is also perfectly opposed to that which is bad or evil or wicked. That's the first point, which must be true for 'good' to have any substance to it. What's more, his opposition is so intense that it's appropriate to call it a *pure* hatred. That's the second point. We may not like the language, but the idea of a 'high intensity' opposition is plain enough. Finally, if there is nothing constraining God from acting on his hatred of evil, *then he will act upon it.*

However, I suspect that even once we've seen the truth of that as it is expressed in Jeremiah's temple sermon, we may not yet be, so to speak, 'feeling the heat' ourselves.

As we saw back in the chapter on Real Outrage, we do have a knack of applying high standards of justice to anyone but ourselves. So I might understand God's anger towards these people 2600 years ago, but I can't understand how he might express the same anger towards me. So let me suggest a couple of ways to bring this home.

The first is to show you how Jesus draws on what we're reading here in Jeremiah to talk of a future expression of God's anger. Let's take a brief look at Jesus' teaching on hell.

Jesus on Hell

In Jeremiah's temple sermon, the name of the valley where the people are sacrificing their children is the Valley of the Sons of Hinnom, sometimes abbreviated to just the Valley of Hinnom. Remember that this becomes the Valley of Slaughter; it's the place where the dead are piled up when God's people experience the full force of his anger. The Hebrew for the Valley of Hinnom is *Ge Hinnom*. In Greek, the language of the New Testament, this becomes *Gehenna*. A word translated in our Bibles as 'hell'.

Six hundred years later than this, in Jesus' time, it was the place where the rubbish from Jerusalem was taken and burnt.

But its association with burning, rotting, death and judgment probably goes back to what we've been reading about in Jeremiah.

Now, however much the idea of hell offends our modern sensibilities, we need to remember that 11 out of the 12 references to hell in the New Testament come from the lips of Jesus himself. And Jesus uses 'hell' as a way of warning what will happen if we fail to turn back to the living God. And his warning is no less severe than Jeremiah's. He warns that insults can make you liable to the fire of hell, that sexual sin can mean the whole body being thrown into hell. The same goes for tempting others to sin, or acting with religious hypocrisy. As he sends out his disciples with the message of the Kingdom, Jesus warns them not to be afraid of being killed by men, but rather

...fear him who can destroy both soul and body in hell.

Hell is much more to be feared than being murdered. You can look that up for yourself in chapter 10 of Matthew's gospel. I've put the other references to Jesus' teaching on hell at the end of this chapter.

But the second way to bring all this home is to see what God is telling us about the Day of the LORD.

The Day of the LORD

This passage from Jeremiah is just one of many graphic passages in the Old Testament that refer to the destruction of Jerusalem in 586BC. That event is the focal point of God's punishment of Israel's unfaithfulness and wickedness in the Old Testament. And it's an act of such decisive punishment that it's called by some of the prophets the 'day of the LORD'—a day when the LORD God visited the world in all his terrifying majesty.

But as with much of what we read in the Old Testament it turns out that the 'day of the LORD' that destroyed Jerusalem was merely a model, a dress-rehearsal for an even more terrifying reality. The Prophets also talk about a 'day of the LORD' that implies a day of universal, cosmic judgment, a day still lying in the future.

It's an idea strongly taken up in the New Testament. Indeed, it is as much an integral part of Jesus' teaching as his teaching on hell. Listen to C. S. Lewis writing in an essay on *The Psalms*:

> The Day of Judgment is an idea very familiar, and very dreadful, to Christians... If there is any concept which cannot by any conjuring be removed from the teaching of Our Lord, it is this of the great separation; the sheep and the goats, the broad way and the narrow, the wheat and the tares, the winnowing fan, the wise and foolish virgins, ... the door closed on the marriage feast, with some inside and some outside in the dark. ... It is from His own words that the picture of 'Doomsday' has come into Christianity.

Now that all authority in heaven and on earth has been given to Jesus, it's the day on which he will judge the world. It's a future event, of unknown timing; a day of great destruction by fire. It will make what we read of in Jeremiah pale into insignificance. It will be the pent-up anger of God, held back for thousands of years, finally released on the world; finally released onto us...

The Shadow of Disaster

Now if all this is true, then we need to be aware of the great instability that exists when God's anger is not yet expressed.

Imagine the following scenario for a disaster movie: A small town lies at the foot of a huge dam. But the dam is unstable and could collapse at any moment.

Fragile dams are something of a cliché in disaster movies. There's a collapsing dam in the truly awful 1970s movie *Earthquake*, and you can even find them in more recent films like *Dante's Peak* and *Hard Rain*. There's a very good example of a collapsing dam scene in *The Two Towers*, the second of Peter Jackson's films of *The Lord of the Rings*. The Ents are marching upon Isengard, enraged by the environmental destruction wrought by the corrupt wizard Saruman. The battle turns when the Ents bring down a huge dam and the enemy is literally washed away. It's a striking scene in a film full of striking images.

But in our movie, the chief engineer at the dam, let's call him the Engineer Jeremy, is warning that it could disintegrate at any moment, sweeping the town away in a tremendous, ferocious flood. And that is rather like our situation as we contemplate God's anger, his righteous opposition to our sin. The righteous anger of God is like a vast lake of water dammed up by a fragile dam. Only God's patience is holding the water back.

I wonder, in our movie, which of the characters would you most identify with?

There is, of course, as in many such movies, the greedy town mayor. Are you perhaps like him? There's a festival due to begin in the town in two days time. The mayor and his business sponsors don't want to lose any money. So they hire experts to say the dam is perfectly safe.

Are you like that when it comes to responding to God's anger at you? You listen to the so-called experts who say there is no hell, that God could never be angry. In Jeremiah's day there were also people, called 'false prophets' by Jeremiah, saying 'Peace, peace,' when there was no peace. Maybe you listen to people like that rather than the true words of God in the Bible because you're so worried about what you might lose. Are you like that?

Disaster movies often also have a stereotypical stubborn old person. The one who refuses to move from his remote and dilapidated house despite the imminent danger. We could have a character like that in our movie. 'I'm not moving for nothin,' they say to anyone sensible who comes by; 'My family have lived in this house for a hundred and fifty years. And we're here to stay—even if it's only me etc. etc.'

Are you perhaps like that? Are you so stuck in your ways that you refuse to even think about what God might feel about your rebellion against him?

Or suppose our movie, like many disaster movies, has a sub-plot. A wild affair, perhaps, between a businessman and his secretary. They're so caught up in each other that they don't recognise the danger until it's too late.

Are you like that? You may not be going so far as adultery. But are you so caught up in and delighting in your sins that you're simply oblivious to how God is going to react to them?

Are you perhaps like the scoundrel in the movie? He also leaves everything until it's too late. He's the one who sees the dam crumbling, leaps into his pick-up truck, speeds past all the people he could be helping, and straight into the nearest lamp-post.

But clichéd and tacky as our movie may be, there is still room for some heroism. Are you the person who sees the danger and does everything they can to get out of the way? Are you the one who not only sees the danger for yourself but also the danger your family is in, the danger your friends are in, the danger your work-colleagues are in? Are you the one who does everything you can to persuade them to get out of the way too?

It's certainly struck me as I've been thinking through this issue that this should radically affect the way we think about those we know who haven't turned back to God. You might like to think about that in the next few days. Take a look around you wherever you are—at work, in the classroom, wherever. Ask yourself: how many of these people actually know about God's righteous anger at their sin? How many of them know the danger they're in?

Now I know every part of us wants to reject that that sort of talk, doesn't it? The modern mind cannot think that such anger could ever be a good thing. We want to consign such talk to the past as too childish, too irrational, and too hot-headed ever to be good.

But hating bad things must by definition be good. This is God's perfect goodness making him perfectly hostile to that which is bad. And we have to face the truth that God's opposition to evil and sin is not a passive opposition, but rather actively expresses itself in amazing and inconceivable fury.

Summary
If we add all that to the picture we have been drawing throughout this book, this is what we get:

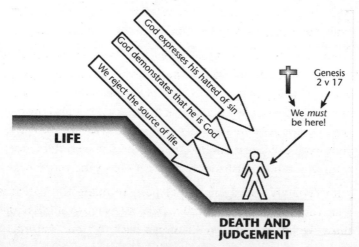

We turn away from and reject the source of life. So we die. We rebel against God and declare him not to be God. He crushes the rebellion, refutes the lie and clears his name. We do what is evil and ugly. He expresses his goodness by acting in punishment against that. God is love, yes. But his love is a just love. He must punish sin.

References to Jesus' teaching on hell: Matthew 5:22, 29-30 (Mark 9:43, 45, 47; Luke 12:5); 10:28; 18:9; 23:15, 33. See also James 3:6.

8 Just Love

WE WOULD LOVE TO THINK our attitude and behaviour towards God doesn't matter. We would love to think that it's OK really, that things will all work out in the end. But everywhere we've turned in the Bible throughout the course of our study, we've found the obvious escape-routes cut off. We say to ourselves: 'surely we can relax, not worry about sin, since God is love.' But no, to understand that God is love depends on understanding his determination to punish sin.

Frantically, we flick through the pages for some other way out. Surely, God can't be *that* concerned by sin? But right at the start of the Bible, we find him solemnly promising to punish sin with death. And we read on, book after book, episode after episode, confirms his determination to punish sin. It is entirely right and appropriate for him to promise to punish it. Like the serpent in the garden, every impulse within us wants to deny it. But he is God, and it's right for him to want to clear his name when it has been defamed by sin. And he is perfectly good. Perfectly opposed to all that is bad.

All the obvious escape routes are cut off. More to the point, the escape routes we tend to rely on are cut off. They are unsafe, positively dangerous even.

But of course there is an escape route. There is a way out. It's an escape route that, again, we may tend to dig our heels in against and resist. Which is so foolish, because it's an escape route guaranteed by God himself and therefore perfectly secure. We've already seen it a number of times in the course of this book. It is to trust in God's Son, Jesus Christ, and to depend on what he has done to save people from the punishment they deserve.

The difference that Jesus makes

We've looked at five principal arguments in this book that God must punish sin, and a number of others besides. He is determined to punish it. And for each of those principal arguments, it is Jesus who confirms that determination. But it is also Jesus who shows us how God can forgive sin, how we can be brought back into a loving relationship with God.

That was perhaps most obvious in the first argument, in the chapter *God is Love*. There we saw how the death of Jesus expressed the ultimate love, taking away from those who trust him the fear of punishment from God on the Day of Judgment. Jesus made all the difference there, and that's true for the other arguments too.

The man who didn't deserve to die

In chapter on *Real Outrage*, we looked at our instinct that rong-doing deserves punishment. We saw that it's an instinct h, while sometimes unreliable, stubbornly refuses to go We saw King David forced to admit by Nathan that he deserved to die. We saw that all of us, no matter how 'modern', 'enlightened' or 'progressive' our views on punishment might be, have an instinctive revulsion against certain things that people do. Our sense of right and wrong may frequently be somewhat faulty, but some crimes simply cry out for justice. The idea that sin deserves the punishment of death is not really so outlandish.

But there has actually been one man who has never in any way deserved to die. It's something that Luke very strongly emphasises in his account of the death of Jesus. Just after he had examined Jesus, the Roman governor Pilate addressed the people who had brought him to trial, offering to release him. This was Pilate's verdict on Jesus: '...I have found in him no guilt deserving death'. But the voices of the crowd prevailed.

And Luke tells us that Jesus was crucified between two criminals. To begin with, they both insulted him. Then one rebuked the other: 'Do you not fear God?' he said, '...we are receiving the due reward of our deeds; but this man has done nothing wrong'. And he turned and said, 'Jesus, remember me when you come into your kingdom'.

We don't know for what crime this man was being executed. We may safely speculate that it wasn't a bit of shop-lifting, given he was undergoing the most extreme form of death penalty possible. This was a man who, were he around today, might well be torn apart publicly by the tabloid press. The sort of man whom, were he to escape the death penalty, would prompt a queue of *Daily Mail* columnists lining up to administer it personally.

Now hear Jesus' utterly astonishing words to him—astonishing given all we've seen throughout this book. Words that promise to bring this man back to the life in all its fullness. The life in the garden that was destroyed by sin and death. This is what Jesus said:

> Truly, I say to you, today you will be with me in Paradise. **Luke 23:43**

The one man who doesn't deserves to die, as he dies the death he doesn't deserve, is able to promise Paradise to the one who confesses he *does* deserve to die, when that person turns to him in trust.

The new Adam

In the chapter on *God is Creator*, we looked at the warning God gave Adam in the garden that sin would be punished by death. We saw that this was no arbitrary command, but rather reflected something foundational about the relationship between God the Creator and his creature.

Now it's true that we weren't there when God declared that command to Adam. It's also true that we express our sin in ways that may have nothing at all to do with trees and serpents. But we live in the same creation. So the relation between sin and punishment, between sin and death, still applies to us. The apostle Paul put it like this:

> ...sin came into the world through one man, and death through sin, and so death spread to all men because all sinned...
> **Romans 5:12**

The link between sin and death was declared to Adam. The link was tragically put into practice when Adam sinned. But we're in the same creation. We're all related to Adam, the representative man in that creation. So the relationship between sin and death applies to us too. He sinned, he died. We sin, we die.

So we can trace a line from that one squalid act of disobedience through the multitude of squalid acts committed by Adam and Eve since, to the universal punishment of death. But then... But then we read on to see Paul comparing this to a radically different act with radically different consequences. He compares Adam to Jesus Christ. Adam's trespass and disobedience to Jesus' perfect obedience. Adam as the precursor of death to Jesus as the precursor of life:

> Therefore, as one trespass led to condemnation for all men, so one act of righteousness leads to justification and life for all men. For as by the one man's disobedience the many were made sinners, so by the one man's obedience the many will be made righteous. **Romans 5 v 18-19**

We need only look to one man, Adam, to make sense of ourselves and why we die. But we need only look to Jesus to rejoice in one man bringing life to many, where once there was death.

The death that demonstrates God's justice

In the chapter on *God is LORD*, we looked at God's determination to refute the lie circulated about him by sin: his determination to clear his name when sin has so defamed it. We also saw why God therefore had to do something radical to demonstrate his justice when he 'passes over' someone's sins. That radical act was the death of his Son on the cross.

But we mustn't also lose sight of the wonderful positive side of that. The amazing thing is that God has found a way of 'passing over' someone's sin and removing the penalty of death. A way that fully demonstrates his authority and justice. And it's through the death of Jesus. Those who have faith in Jesus have the penalty of death removed as a gift. Once again the supreme love and generosity of God shines out. As Paul himself puts it...

> ...while we were still weak, at the right time Christ died for the ungodly. For one will scarcely die for a righteous person – though perhaps for a good person one would dare even to die – but God

shows his love for us in that while we were still sinners, Christ died for us. **Romans 5:6-8**

The man who delivers us from God's wrath

In the chapter *God is Good*, we dwelt on God's perfect goodness making him perfectly hostile to that which is bad. We faced up to the truth that God's opposition to evil and sin is not a passive opposition, but rather actively expresses itself in amazing and unimaginable fury.

Our situation is like living at the foot of a dam on the verge of collapse, at risk at any moment of sweeping us away in a tremendous, ferocious flood.

Now imagine something still more amazing and inconceivable. Imagine that the threat were simply taken away. Not by repressing it, or ignoring it or arrogantly dismissing it, which of course would do nothing to take it away. But really taken away. For free—as an undeserved gift. That would be something worth having, wouldn't it? That would be a life-changing moment: something to sing and shout about.

And we start to understand why the apostle Paul is so full of thanksgiving and praise as he writes to the church of the Thessalonians. Because they have 'turned to God from idols to serve the true and living God'; and they're waiting 'for his Son from heaven, whom he raised from the dead—Jesus, who delivers us from the wrath to come'.

God wants you to know that the threat against you is a real one. But the solution is also a real one: to turn and serve the true and living God, trusting in Jesus, who delivers us from the wrath to come.

Galatians chapter 2, verse 20

People squabble. Even in the groups of people saying they have aligned themselves with Jesus Christ, people squabble. It's not pretty, but it has always been so. You only have to read Paul's letters in the New Testament to see just how true that is.

But resolving squabbles can give birth to great insights. And that is very true in Paul's letter to the Christians in Galatia. In tackling a rather messy and complicated squabble, Paul gives us a beautiful summary of difference the death of Jesus makes for those who trust him.

Roughly speaking, the squabble was this: On one side were people saying that to truly be one of God's people you have to align yourself to the heritage of God's people, which is a way of life based around the 'Law'.

But what is this 'Law'?

We've been saying throughout this book that God must punish sin—ultimately, with death. This is what Paul calls elsewhere the 'law of sin and death'. It is the 'law', or warning, given by God to Adam: if you sin, then you die.

What we haven't yet looked at is that God said that again when he gave his people the 'Law', capital L, through Moses. He said it in a much more elaborate, precise and historically specific way. In the Law, there are rules to make Israel distinctive as a nation. There are rules of sacrifice. These things are quite particular to their situation. But, essentially, it was the same message. The 'law of sin and death' is also right at the heart of the Law, capital L, given to Moses for the Israelites on mount Sinai, a thousand odd years before Christ. This, very precisely now, is what it means to sin. If you sin, you will be punished—ultimately, with death. With exclusion from the presence of God.

Now, says Paul, to be part of a people who received God's 'Law' may well be a great privilege. In many ways, that's a noble heritage. *But it's not the thing that gives you life with God—* it cannot be! On the contrary, says Paul, those with access to the Law should know more than anyone, in exhaustive detail, *how much* they deserve death.

We said in the last chapter that living as one who has sinned is like living at the foot of an unsafe, crumbling dam. In such a situation, mere possession of something like the 'Law' is little help on its own. It's no more useful than living at the foot at that dam and having access to the best construction plans— perhaps even a first-class engineering degree to understand them. You might well have a better idea than those around you when and where the dam will collapse. But if that's all you're relying on, you'll be swept away with them nonetheless.

No, the only way to life, says Paul, is through death. How so? Listen carefully to what he says:

> I have been crucified with Christ. It is no longer I who live, but Christ who lives in me. And the life I now live in the flesh I live by faith in the Son of God, who loved me and gave himself for me.
> **Galatians 2 v 20**

This is what matters! God must punish your sin—ultimately, with death. But look at this: What if you align yourself—not with a cultural heritage or a legal system—but with Jesus Christ? What if you unite yourself to him, trust him, believe in him? And, so united to him, you die with him, in him? Now there's a way out!

Throughout this book, we've been building up a very depressing picture, gradually adding more and more reasons why God must punish our sin. But just look how that picture is transformed when we add the good news of the death and resurrection of Jesus:

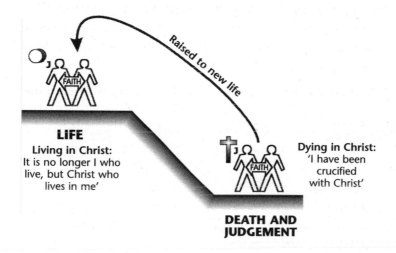

Because of our sins, we deserve to die. But life is possible because of Jesus Christ. We can break free from the law of sin and death if we unite ourselves to him by faith. And faith is the key. That committed trust in Jesus, which Paul describes elsewhere as being like a marriage commitment, is what can unite us to Jesus, and gain us the benefits of both his death and resurrection.

So Paul can say: 'I have been crucified with Christ' – I have died in him. And he can say, 'It is no longer I (my sinful self) who lives, but Christ who lives in me'. That's the way out. Indeed, Paul goes on to say, the only way out, unless 'Christ died for no purpose'. That trust, that 'faith in the Son of God', really can give you life with God as one of his treasured people.

The final impact

We've looked at a number of arguments that suggest God must punish our sin with death. As we've also looked at what sin is, you may have become more aware of your own sin. However, my main aim has been to show you that, whether you're aware of your sin or not, you deserve to die, and that that is God's verdict on you. It's an uncomfortable truth, but it's a truth that should have a deep impact on all of us.

If you were suddenly to discover you had a terminal illness, that would probably stop you in your tracks. Most of us have friends or family members who have been through that trauma. It knocks people flat—not surprisingly. But this is more severe news even than that—and more universal. This has not been some interesting, intellectual debate on the character of God. This is personal.

God must punish sin. And as we finish, let's begin to look at the final impact of that.

Living by faith in the Son of God

Now of course there's an obvious implication for anyone reading this who does not yet trust in Jesus. You know what you have to do. Given all that God has told us about his character through the Bible passages we have looked at, you should know in great detail now why he must punish your sin with death. You know the danger you're in. And you should also know the way out, which is to submit yourself to Jesus, who will die for your sins on your behalf, so that you might live and not face God's anger.

And I suggest you act urgently.

C. S. Lewis describes the experience of being brought by God to trust in Jesus Christ as living for a time like a hunted animal.

'Amiable agnostics will talk cheerfully about "man's search for God",' he said; 'To me, as I then was, they might just as well have talked about the mouse's search for the cat'.

And if, after all we've talked about through these pages, you're still wanting to deny that God must punish sin, I do hope you're feeling a bit like that mouse. You're cornered. It's time for surrender.

Because the extraordinary thing is that for those who have faith in Jesus, God has provided a way to demonstrate his authority, his justice and his hatred of sin in such a way that he can pass over their sins and forgive them.

I'm told on good authority by lifesaving experts that if you're drowning, the recommended action if someone throws you a lifeline is to grab it and hold on very, very tightly.

If you have a life-threatening illness and there's some treatment that will save you, I understand that current medical advice is that you take the medicine or submit to the knife.

Now I know I've not been recounting palatable truths throughout this book. But God is telling us that he does intend to refute the lies we tell about him every time we sin. And wise advice, I think, would be to take hold of the solution he provides. If you're not someone whom Paul would describe as 'one who has faith in Jesus', it would be sensible, would it not, to look into doing that?

And if you're starting to see just how much your sin deserves punishment, you may also be starting to see just how amazing God's love must be. He has provided a way for your sins to be punished. But he has done it at the highest personal cost—by sending his Son to die. It's such an amazing act of love that it defines what love is. Just think—you could be on the receiving end of that. You could be caught up in the most wonderful expression of love ever.

You know what you have to do. But not, perhaps, exactly how to do it. One thing you could do is turn back to the words of the second thief on the cross we looked at a few pages ago (they're on page 112 or in Luke, chapter 23, verses 40 to 42). Why not say to God something similar? Say something like, 'I know I'm guilty, that I deserve to die. I can see that Jesus alone has the authority and ability to help me. I need his love. I need his help'. If you say that to God, and mean it, then Jesus' promise of a restored life is for you too.

Telling others

For those of us who would say we are trusting Jesus, I hope too there are obvious implications for telling people about the rescue he provides. First, for the urgency to warn others, which has been made very clear. If our friends, family, colleagues and acquaintances are like people living at the foot of a crumbling dam, then surely the determination to tell them about life through Jesus should be enormous. What a cold and casual lack of concern it would be to leave them in the dark!

But the other way in which our lives should be affected is this: Unless we tell people God must punish their sins, and why, we really haven't told them the full story. It's all very well telling people about the blessings of the Christian life, and especially the blessing of an eternal relationship with the living God. But if we somehow omit to tell the most compelling reason they should turn back to God and believe the great news of Jesus Christ's victory over death, then we are doing them no favours. And we bring glory to God when we proclaim his authority and goodness and justice. So let's not pussy-foot around: let's not be ashamed to do just that.

The Seriousness of Sin

God must punish sin. Perhaps less obvious is the impact this truth should have on our everyday walk with God. For example, think about your attitude to sin. People hearing about Jesus Christ for the first time often wonder, given that life through him is a free gift, what the incentive could be to stop sinning. Well, there are many answers to that. But here's one of them.

Given all we've seen over the last eight chapters, think about just how much God hates sin. Can we really go on thoughtlessly sinning knowing that?

When I was seven, I remember a boy, a bit younger than me, coming to play who had a peculiar obsession with mud and collecting earthworms. It really was the most extraordinary thing to see. He would go around the garden collecting great handfuls of worms. It was also rather gruesome to watch, because he held onto them tightly, which did cause them to disintegrate somewhat. Despite this, earthworms (you may be interested to know) are surprisingly hard to kill, so there was plenty of wriggling still going on. He would come in from the garden simply covered from head to foot in mud, blood and bits of worm. All over his hands and arms, all over his clothes, all over his face.

Now he grew up perfectly normal, so far as I know, and doesn't do that any more. And I imagine one of the reasons he gave it up was the reaction of sheer horrified revulsion and disgust he managed to provoke in anyone who witnessed it—especially his poor mother, who was almost beside herself.

As we grow up we take cues from our parents as to what is and what isn't acceptable. That's true for all of us, even if not all of us, thankfully, have obsessions with earthworms. But shouldn't we be all the more taking cues from our Heavenly Father?

Next time you know you're just about commit a sin, just stop and think about that. Think about the intensity with which God hates the thing you're just about to do. Go back to the Bible. Just feel the intensity and heat of the language he uses to express his hatred of the sorts of things you're about to do. Look at the cross. The horror of it! God hates the thing you are about to so much that he was prepared to send his only Son to die to deal with it.

The motivation to love

Following on from that, let's take another example. Think about your motivation to love. Remember back to the chapter *God is Love* and John's agenda in reminding us of Jesus' death? John wants us to know and understand God's love for us better and better. And he wants us to behave accordingly, as God's children. And as we love our brothers and sisters in Christ, he wants us to have that deep assurance that we are indeed children of God.

But to know all that, we also need to know that apart from Christ we deserve to die. We deserve to be punished, but he was punished on our behalf, demonstrating God's justice and authority, expressing his hatred of sin.

The more we understand and experience that, John tells us, the more we will understand God's love, and the more able we are to express true love ourselves. The visible test of whether we understand God's character, his love and his justice, will be whether we ourselves are motivated by that to act in love to those around us.

Who would have thought that believing in punishment for sins would in the end make Christians more loving, not less?

Enjoying God's love

Finally, as we think about this, let's dwell deeply on God's love for us. And not just dwell on it—enjoy it! Experience it! We live in a world which yearns deeply for genuine love. Each of us, to some extent, is a love-sick child. But the person who trusts Jesus and is convinced of God's justice has access to the most precious thing in the world. It's at the heart of a strong relationship with our Heavenly Father. It's the definitive expression of love and it's ours to experience and enjoy.

So, I don't know, perhaps you've been thinking it rather morbid and gratuitous to dedicate a whole book to how God must punish sin. It's unlikely that you've found it a fun use of time to be told repeatedly that God is not 'just love', but that his love is a just love and that he must punish sin. But if we're serious about our relationship with God, perhaps this sober truth should be right at the heart of what we believe.

And perhaps our reluctance to admit that our sins deserve punishment does stem, in part, from our desperate desire to be loved by God. If so, it is my hope and prayer that the things we have talked about in this book will help us see just how wrongheaded that is. The greatest love of God is poured out as he deals with sins that deserve death. By humbling ourselves and admitting our need for forgiveness we can be on the receiving end of that. In the end, the riches of the whole world are nothing compared to that love. That such love is freely available to us all is surely the best news in the world.

Appendix

The Parable of the Unforgiving Servant

Throughout this book, we've seen that there must be more to forgiving sin than simply cancelling a debt. But when we turn to chapter 18 of Matthew's gospel, the two ideas do seem to be very closely tied together. (Similar things could be said of the much shorter parable Jesus tells Simon the Pharisee in Luke chapter 7.) This is the 'parable of the unforgiving servant' in full:

> Then Peter came up and said to him, 'Lord, how often will my brother sin against me, and I forgive him? As many as seven times?' Jesus said to him, 'I do not say to you seven times, but seventy times seven.

> 'Therefore the kingdom of heaven may be compared to a king who wished to settle accounts with his servants. When he began to settle, one was brought to him who owed him ten thousand talents. And since he could not pay, his master ordered him to be sold, with his wife and his children and all that he had, and payment to be made. So the servant fell on his knees, imploring him, "Have patience with me, and I will pay you everything." And out of pity for him, the master of the servant released him and forgave him the debt. But when that same servant went out, he found one of his fellow servants who owed him a hundred denarii, and seizing him, he began to choke him, saying, "Pay

what you owe." So his fellow servant fell down and pleaded with him, "Have patience with me, and I will pay you." He refused and went and put him in prison until he should pay the debt. When his fellow servants saw what had taken place, they were greatly distressed, and they went and reported to their master all that had taken place. Then his master summoned him and said to him, "You wicked servant! I forgave you all that debt because you pleaded with me. And should not you have mercy on your fellow servant, as I had mercy on you?" And in his anger his master delivered him to the jailers, until he should pay his debt. So also my heavenly Father will do to every one of you, if you do not forgive your brother from the heart.' **Matthew 18:21-35**

Let me first say a few words about making generalisations from parables. The means by which God forgives sin is complex and it's very unlikely that any one parable is going to capture every aspect of the reality. Parables are not allegories: we do not see a one-to-one correspondence between the details of a parable and the details of the reality they illustrate. What we tend to see is the parable making just a few simple points (sometimes only one).

In this case we can easily see the purpose of the parable. Peter wants to know how many times he should forgive a brother who sins against him. The purpose of the parable is to persuade Peter (and us) that his forgiveness should be unlimited. Jesus achieves that purpose with it by telling a story about a master, a servant and one of the servant's fellow servants. The master forgives the servant a huge debt. The servant then fails to forgive his fellow servant a much smaller debt. The master then punishes him for his wickedness. We can feel in the story how incongruous the unforgiving servant's behaviour has been. And Jesus tells us that there are sufficient parallels between this story and the relation between God's forgiveness of us and our forgiveness of our brothers to make unforgiveness incongruous for us too.

Now someone convinced that the essence of sin is a debt to God might say this: Look, we are being asked to forgive others their debts to us because God has forgiven our debts. The two are tied together very closely in the parable. But when we forgive someone their debts to us, we just do it—we just let it go. We don't insist on the debt being paid—by, say, some third party. So the same must be true when God forgives us.

However, that is a very difficult line of argument to sustain. To start with, although there's a parallel in the story between the debt forgiven by the master and the debt not forgiven by the servant, there is also a clear distinction. The debt forgiven by the master is 10,000 talents. A talent represented perhaps twenty years wages for a labourer. This is distinctly marked out in the account as an uncommon, almost unreal, debt compared with the relatively trifling amount owed to the servant. We should hesitate before saying that the master should 'just let it go'. There was clearly a huge personal cost to him in cancelling it.

Moreover, why exactly was the servant's behaviour 'wicked'? We're not told explicitly, though we can see his lack of sympathy with someone in a parallel situation. We see enough to get the point. But was it wicked because it's intrinsically wrong not to forgive debts? If we're expected to make a strong parallel between the two debts, that would mean the master would also have been wrong not to forgive. Both master and servant would have been morally obligated to forgive. Which would be odd. In that case, it would be odd to talk of them being 'owed' anything.

More likely what's going on is this: The way we have treated God is much, much worse than the way anyone has treated us. And yet, if we're a follower of Jesus, he has forgiven us. If we refuse to forgive someone, then it's like saying, 'You know, God, I don't think you should have forgiven me. Especially since what you forgave was so much more than this. *If I were you, I wouldn't have done it.*'

In other words, to fail to forgive when you have been forgiven by God is to cast aspersions on his justice in forgiving you. And as we saw in the chapter on *God is LORD*, the lie that God is unjust is one he is determined to refute. Indeed, he is determined to clear his name of such slander by acting in punishment. Which is a determination supported by what happens to the servant at the end of this parable.

This understanding of the parable is in accord with teaching on forgiveness elsewhere in the Bible, and picked up by the apostle Paul:

> Beloved, never avenge yourselves, but leave it to the wrath of God, for it is written, 'Vengeance is mine, I will repay, says the LORD'. **Romans 12 v 19**

As individuals in God's creation, we are commanded to forgive rather as someone might write off a debt—that is certainly true. But that does not mean God is similarly obliged to. Ultimately, justice is his business.